teach
yourself

allotment gardening

allotment gardening
geoff stokes

Launched in 1938, the **teach yourself** series grew rapidly in response to the world's wartime needs. Loved and trusted by over 50 million readers, the series has continued to respond to society's changing interests and passions and now, 70 years on, includes over 500 titles, from Arabic and Beekeeping to Yoga and Zulu. What would you like to learn?

be where you want to be with **teach yourself**

For order enquiries please contact Bookpoint Ltd, 130 Milton Park, Abingdon, Oxon OX14 4SB. Telephone: +44 (0) 1235 827720. Fax: +44 (0) 1235 400454. Lines are open 09.00–17.00, Monday to Saturday, with a 24-hour message answering service. Details about our titles and how to order are available at www.teachyourself.co.uk

Long renowned as the authoritative source for self-guided learning – with more than 50 million copies sold worldwide – the **teach yourself** series includes over 500 titles in the fields of languages, crafts, hobbies, business, computing and education.

British Library Cataloguing in Publication Data: a catalogue record for this title is available from the British Library.

First published in UK 2009 by Hodder Education, part of Hachette UK, 338 Euston Road, London NW1 3BH.

This edition published 2009.

The **teach yourself** name is a registered trademark of Hodder Headline.

Copyright © 2009 Geoff Stokes

Typeset by Transet Ltd, Coventry.
Printed in Great Britain for Hodder Education, an Hachette UK Company, 338 Euston Road, London NW1 3BH, by CPI Cox & Wyman, Reading, Berkshire RG1 8EX.

The publisher has used its best endeavours to ensure that the URLs for external websites referred to in this book are correct and active at the time of going to press. However, the publisher and the author have no responsibility for the websites and can make no guarantee that a site will remain live or that the content will remain relevant, decent or appropriate.

Hachette UK's policy is to use papers that are natural, renewable and recyclable products and made from wood grown in sustainable forests. The logging and manufacturing processes are expected to conform to the environmental regulations of the country of origin.

Impression number	10 9 8 7 6 5 4 3 2 1
Year	2012 2011 2010 2009

contents

dedication

To my wife Liz, son David and daughter Jennifer for their support, encouragement (and endurance) during my 20 years' service with the allotment movement.

acknowledgements

I would like to thank the current and past officers and members of the National Society of Allotment and Leisure Gardeners, without whom my job would have been less enjoyable.

introduction

The right use of leisure is said to be one of the greatest problems of modern times. If by this is meant the use of leisure hours in the most profitable way, both for oneself and the community, then gardening ranks very high, giving as it does bodily health, mental relaxation and a good return for the money and energy expended, as well as being an abounding source of interest. The cumulative effect of this is to make life more tolerable for a great number of people whose opportunities for health giving activities and pleasures might be extremely limited.

Extract from 'Gardening Associations: How to Form and Run Them', The National Society of Allotment and Leisure Gardeners Ltd

This book is for people new to or recently introduced to growing their own food. It aims to provide an understanding of the basic principles of vegetable growing and the issues involved in taking on an allotment plot. The book also includes information and top tips to aid the more experienced gardener and those wishing to grow their own food at home.

The book is intended to guide rather than to dictate which gardening methods or principles to follow. The methods you choose must suit your own abilities, skills and growing conditions. Vegetable growing and gardening in general are activities that teach new things all the time, so you are constantly learning and honing your skills.

Vegetable growing is extremely rewarding both in terms of the fresh wholesome produce grown and in the sense of achievement of producing something from seed.

The seed and plant varieties mentioned in this book have been selected because they are available from several seed companies, and are reliable at cropping. The 'Author's choice' sections in Chapter 05 reflect varieties grown by the author that have produced consistent results on his plot.

Basic cooking instructions have been included for each vegetable variety to help you to get the best out of the crop (Chapter 05), together with some simple recipes to make the most out of your produce (Chapter 11).

01

what is an allotment?

In the UK, 'allotments' were originally parcels of land up to 2 ha (5 acres) in area (about the size of three football pitches) that were let to 'commoners' and the landless poor as a result of the Enclosure Awards 1760–1818 when some 2 million ha (5 million acres) of common land was enclosed and passed into private ownership. This action, which was supported by the UK Government through various Acts of Parliament, prevented the 'common' people from gathering fuel, grazing their animals and gathering food from the land that they previously had a right to use.

In the late 1800s, allotments were seen as a way of keeping the labouring poor out of the workhouse by allowing them to grow their own food, and in doing so they did not need parish relief. Legislation was enacted that required councils to provide allotments where they were not provided by charitable benefactors such as the church.

In 1908, all previous allotment legislation was consolidated and for the first time local authorities became obliged to provide a sufficient number of allotments for use by their parishioners where there was a demand for them. This obligation to provide allotments is still in force today.

In 1922, following the drive for the nation to grow and provide more food in the First World War, and with the shortage of available land due to land that had been requisitioned for food growing being returned to its owners, the demand for allotments grew and the UK Government introduced a new category of 'allotment gardens'. These were areas of land, restricted in size to a maximum of 40 poles (1,000 sq m/1,200 sq yards), to be used wholly or mainly for the cultivation of vegetable or fruit crops for consumption by the occupier and his or her family.

However, this did not prevent local authorities from continuing to provide allotments if they wished, but in 1950 legislation was introduced which restricted the obligation of local authorities to the provision of allotment gardens only. Local authorities with a population over 10,000 were also obliged to provide allotment gardens not exceeding 20 pole (500 sq m/600 sq yards). Currently, the standard size of an allotment plot is 250 sq m (300 sq yards), and this is what most councils provide.

Where there is a high demand for plots, some councils are now reducing plot sizes to 125 sq m (150 sq yards), but such action is seen by allotment gardeners as a 'false economy'.

Nevertheless, it is believed that a variety of plots – standard, half, or even quarter plots – could, or should, be made available for use by smaller families or single people where a larger plot might be too big for their needs.

In the major cities in the UK, allotment plots might not be readily available because of high demand and shortage of plots and available land. This is particularly so in the inner London boroughs where the power to provide allotments is discretionary and not compulsory.

Why have an allotment?

An allotment could be the answer for you if you have concerns about:

- the rising cost of food
- the use of chemicals and additives in food to enhance flavour, add colour or preserve and prolong shelf life
- the distance food travels from where it is grown to when it reaches the local supermarket or greengrocer and your plate.

In addition, if you wish to improve your family's diet with the addition of fresh fruit and vegetables or if you simply do not have a garden or your garden is too small for vegetable growing, then an allotment is a possible solution.

Allotment gardening has been a popular activity for over 150 years, from its origins of providing food for the labouring and landless poor by subsistence farming, through the 'Dig for Victory' campaign of the war years and its heyday in post-war Britain, to the present day where it is an activity enjoyed by people from all walks of society. Allotment gardening provides an opportunity for the individual or family to grow fresh, healthy food in abundance, knowing where it has come from and exactly how it has been grown. Today, allotment gardening is an increasingly popular pastime, and quite rightly so!

Allotment gardening offers many benefits:

- The health benefits of regular and prolonged exercise using a wide group of muscles.
- The social benefits of meeting and sharing an activity with like-minded people.
- The environmental benefits of participating in a sustainable activity and learning about working with nature.

More importantly, it helps to retain a 'little bit of green space' and nature in our urban areas for future generations to enjoy. At a planning public enquiry in Northampton in 1990, the planning inspector described an allotment site as 'a green oasis in an otherwise urban sprawl', and this applies to many if not most allotment sites throughout the country.

Growing your own fruit and vegetables also enables you to control the use of chemical pesticides and weedkillers so that you know exactly with what, if anything, your crops have been treated.

Vegetables contain many of the essential vitamins that we all need, but the content depends on how fresh the produce is. As soon as crops are harvested, the vitamin content starts to reduce, so by growing and harvesting your own vegetables, and eating them fresh, you can be sure you are getting the most from the vitamin content available. Freezing surplus fresh vegetables will also assist in retaining the vitamin content.

How much produce can be grown on a plot?

In 1975, a trial allotment plot managed by students at the Royal Horticultural Society gardens at Harlow Carr, Yorkshire, produced vegetable and fruit crops with a value at that time in excess of £240. At today's supermarket prices, the same crops would be valued at £1,500, but if you wish to be entirely organic the value would be higher. The students spent 180 hours in total between March and November working on the plot, which is the equivalent of about five hours' work per week.

It should be possible for any allotment gardener to achieve similar results, but this will depend on whether you are growing crops with a high or low value or yield; however, there are also the added benefits to your health and the environment to take into consideration.

A standard size allotment garden should be sufficient for a family of four to provide a reasonable proportion of their annual vegetable and fruit needs. It is unlikely that a standard size plot will be large enough to enable the plotholder to be entirely self-sufficient, as this would require at least 1,000 sq m (1,200 sq yards), which is more than most councils are now obliged to provide.

To get the best results from the plot, keep sowing and planting throughout the growing season, to fill any gaps as crops are harvested.

Allotments can also be used to keep livestock, such as hens, rabbits, pigs and goats, and this is dealt with in more detail in Chapter 08.

The more time you have available to tend your plot, the better the results will be.

What costs are involved in running an allotment plot?

Costs will vary depending on your needs. The expenditure for some items, such as tools, pots and seed trays, will not be required every year as the equipment should last for several seasons if taken care of.

Approximate costs:

- Rent £35 per annum.
- Seeds £30–50 per annum.
- Water £5 per annum.
- Compost £10 per annum.
- Fertilizer £10 per annum.
- Pots and seed trays £10 per annum.

The average annual cost is £112, plus £60–80 for basic tools.

How much time is required to manage a plot?

The more time you have available to spend on your plot the more you will be able to achieve and produce. You should consider the equivalent of half an hour of work per day on your plot as the minimum time required to achieve reasonable results. You should visit your plot at least once a week otherwise weeds and pests will take hold and these can affect other plots as well as your own crops.

When taking holidays, ask another plotholder or friend to keep an eye on your plot to ensure that crops do not dry out, and maturing crops are picked to encourage continuing cropping.

If asking a friend, you may need to let others on the site know the arrangements you have made.

If your time is limited, think about planting low maintenance crops, such as potatoes, onions and root crops, and avoid crops that require harvesting every couple of days such as beans, lettuce and courgettes.

You might also consider sharing a plot, and the work, with a friend or neighbour.

Go on – get an allotment – you'll love it!

02

obtaining a plot

In this chapter you will learn:
- who provides allotments
- what the annual rent is
- what the terms of allotment tenancies are.

Who provides allotment plots?

In view of the legal requirement in the UK for local authorities to provide allotments, most allotments are owned and run by the local council. This will be a parish or town council where these exist or the district council where there is no parish council.

In the first instance, you can contact your local council for a list of sites within the area, and to obtain details of availability, waiting lists, rent and other relevant matters. Some sites are privately owned and administered, and your local library may be able to help you find a contact for them, although sometimes the best way to locate them is by speaking to neighbours who might point you in the right direction.

Top tip

Many councils (particularly district) have websites that will enable you to find information about their allotment provision. If you are unsure as to which council covers your area, visit **www.direct.gov.uk** where you can find the relevant council by keying in your postcode.

Top tip

If you have access to the Internet, look at the aerial views of your town on **www.google.co.uk/earth**. Allotment sites are easy to distinguish from other land use by their rectangular plots and paths.

If there are no allotments in the parish or district, six resident parliamentary electors or ratepayers need to write to the council requesting an allotment – this then places a duty on the council to take such representations into consideration. If the council refuses to make provision, it leaves itself open to a legal challenge. A complaint could be made to the local government ombudsman if a borough or district council fails to make any provision without a valid reason. Alternatively, contact your local ward councillor and/or Member of Parliament (MP) and seek their support for the provision of such a facility. If all else fails, ask the local press to get involved to support your campaign for adequate provision of allotments.

Costs

Rent levels vary from county to county, and also from site to site, and can range from £3 to £100 per year. The current national average is approximately £25–35 per annum, but the amount of rent charged will usually depend on what facilities, if any, are available to the plotholder or site such as water, car parking, security fencing, rubbish removal, toilets or a communal building. The more facilities provided, the higher the rent is likely to be. Councils are not legally obliged to provide any facilities, and consequently many provide nothing other than the land.

Where a council provides more than one allotment site, try to visit several and speak to people on the sites to see how well crops grow and whether there have ever been any problems with vandalism, trespassers, flooding, and so on, and also what facilities are available.

Assuming there are several plots available for rent, the ideal would be south facing with good, free-draining soil, sheltered from northerly winds, with a nearby water supply. However, most soils can be brought into good fertility with a little time and effort and the addition of compost or manure. Avoid plots that are next to weedy overgrown hedges or overshadowed by trees.

If a site is well tenanted and cultivated, and appears lively, this can be a sign of a well-run and productive site. However, if there is a high demand for plots your choice may be limited and you may have to compromise.

Many sites have formed active associations that offer their members the use of a trading hut; hold regular meetings; hold allotment competitions; and have fund-raising events. Consequently, renting an allotment can be an excellent way to meet new people, and to become part of your local community.

Allotment tenancies

The relationship created by the use of land as an allotment garden is that of landlord and tenant, whereby the tenant enters into a legal contract to rent the plot and agrees to observe a number of terms and conditions. The tenant then has exclusive possession of the plot for a fixed term and for a set rent.

It is always better to have a written tenancy agreement as this ensures that the tenant is aware of the conditions of the tenancy. Make sure you receive a copy of the agreement from the landlord for your records. If you are not given a copy, ask for one.

Verbal tenancies are legally acceptable and binding, but can be harder to enforce in the event of problems occurring since it will be difficult for either party to prove exactly what terms they had agreed to.

Terms of tenancy

Tenancies are usually granted on an annual basis and are renewable or continue in force until such time as they are terminated by either the landlord or tenant.

Legislation requires some terms to be included in tenancy agreements, such as the length of notice required to terminate a tenancy, but the landlord is also allowed to make such other rules as they think necessary for the management of the allotments, providing these are not contrary to the legislation.

Tenancy agreements normally include the following clauses in their terms and conditions:

1 The date on which the rent is due to be paid.

   (Rent is payable at the beginning of the tenancy, but the annual rent day might differ.)

2 The Tenant shall use the plot as an Allotment Garden only and for no other purpose, and to keep it clean and free from weeds and in a good state of cultivation and fertility and in good condition.

   (An allotment garden is not intended to be used by way of trade or business, but the current view is that this would not prevent the sale or disposal of surplus produce.)

3 The Tenant shall not cause any inconvenience or annoyance to the occupier of any other allotment garden, or obstruct any path set out by the council for the use of the occupiers of the allotment gardens.

4 The Tenant shall not sub-let or part with the possession of the allotment garden or any part thereof without the written consent of the Council.

   (An allotment garden is intended for use by the tenant only

and cannot be passed on to someone else without the landlord's approval and permission.)

5 The Tenant shall not, without the written consent of the Council, cut or prune any timber or other trees, or take, sell or carry away any mineral, sand or clay.

(The soil and any trees or hedges on the allotment [other than those planted by the tenant] belong to the landowner and consequently the tenant does not have any right to dispose of such materials without permission.)

6 The Tenant shall not keep livestock on the allotment other than that permitted by law without the prior written consent of the council.

(The 1950 Allotment Act allows allotment garden tenants to keep hens and rabbits as a right, provided such animals are not kept in a condition as to be prejudicial to health, or cause a nuisance.

While there is nothing in law to prevent other livestock, such as pigs, goats and bees, being kept on an allotment garden, this can only be done with the express approval of the landlord.)

7 The Tenant shall keep every hedge that forms part of the boundary of his/her allotment garden properly cut and trimmed, keep all ditches properly cleansed and maintained and keep in repair any other fences and any other gates or sheds on his allotment.

(This clause requires the tenant to keep the boundary of their plot tidy and well maintained.)

8 The Tenant shall not use barbed wire for a fence adjoining any path put by the Council for the use of the occupiers of the allotment gardens.

(This clause is aimed at preventing accidental injury to third parties for which the tenant would otherwise be legally liable.)

9 The Tenant shall not without the written consent of the Council erect any building on the allotment garden, and shall be responsible for the removal of any building on or before the expiry of the tenancy.

(The landlord has a legal right to determine what buildings, if any, it is prepared to allow on the plot and to determine what size and from what materials they are constructed.

It is thought reasonable for a landlord to allow a tool shed, greenhouse and polytunnel to be erected, since these can enhance the use of the plot.)

10 The Tenant shall, as regards the allotment gardens, observe and perform all conditions and covenants set out in the lease under which the council holds the land.

(Where a council itself leases land from another owner, the tenant is required to observe and comply with the terms of that lease as well as their own tenancy agreement. It is advisable under such circumstances to obtain a copy of any relevant clauses.)

11 Any member or Officer of the Council shall be entitled at any time when directed by the Council, to enter and inspect the allotment garden.

12 The tenancy of the allotment garden shall terminate on the yearly rent day after the death of the tenant and shall also terminate whenever the tenancy or right of occupation of the Council terminates. It may also be terminated by the Council by re-entry after one month's notice:

i   if the rent is in arrears for not less than 40 days or
ii   if the Tenant is not duly observing the conditions of his/her tenancy or
iii if he/she becomes bankrupt or compounds with his/her creditors.

The tenancy may also be terminated by the Council or Tenant by 12 months' previous notice in writing expiring on or before 6 April or on or after 29 September in any year.

(These requirements for termination of an allotment garden tenancy are to be found in the Allotment Acts 1908–1950.)

13 The Tenant shall on entry pay the Stamp Duty on this agreement and also pay any compensation payable to the outgoing tenant for crops or improvements.

(Currently, Stamp Duty is not payable unless the contract is for a term of more than seven years, and exceeds £100 rental.

An incoming tenant may be liable for compensation for growing crops or buildings belonging to the outgoing tenant. However, if the incoming tenant does not require the crops or buildings it is the responsibility of the outgoing tenant to remove his/her property before the expiry of the notice terminating the tenancy.)

14 Rates in respect of the allotment garden shall be paid by
....

(Allotment gardens are presently treated as agricultural land and therefore rates are not payable.)

Important!

It is a tenant's responsibility to keep the plot in a good state of fertility and cultivation, which effectively means free of weeds, and to keep the plot boundary hedges cut and trimmed and ditches free from rubbish.

Ensure that you check the terms of your tenancy agreement as you may need to obtain permission before carrying out activities such as erecting a shed or greenhouse or, for example, if you wish to mulch with old carpets or light bonfires.

Frequently asked questions

- *Can the council stop me from keeping livestock?* Yes, for anything other than hens and rabbits.
- *Does the council have any control over what produce I grow?* Generally no, but it might wish to limit the number or size of fruit trees planted on the plot.
- *When can the council terminate a tenancy?* Tenancies can be terminated with one month's notice if the tenant fails to pay the rent or does not comply with the tenancy terms. Otherwise, 12 months' notice is required.
- *Must I cultivate the whole plot?* You should be cultivating a large part of the plot, but any uncultivated area must be kept weed-free.
- *What happens if I miss paying the rent?* The landlord should send out rent reminders when the rent is due for renewal, but if you fail to make payment your tenancy is liable to be terminated. If you think you might have problems paying the rent on time, let your landlord know as soon as possible.

03

getting started

In this chapter you will learn:
- how to clear a neglected plot
- how to identify soil types
- what manures and fertilizers are
- how to plan and work your plot.

Clearing a neglected plot

It would be very unusual to be given an allotment plot that is already clean, tidy and well cultivated. Most vacant plots tend to have been neglected and consequently may be full of overgrown weeds. Do not let this put you off as the soil, once cleared, can still be very productive.

Ideally, you should take on a plot in the autumn as this allows the plot to be cleared over the whole of the winter, but you may not have the choice as it will depend on when a plot becomes available.

The ultimate aim in clearing a plot is to remove every trace of weeds, including the roots, to leave a clean soil. This can prove to be a lengthy operation for which the use of a rotovator is not always practical. Perennial weeds, such as brambles, buttercup, couch grass, docks, dandelions, ground elder, nettles and mare's tail, need to be removed completely as they will regenerate from any small fragment of root left in the ground.

Annual weeds, which include groundsel, chickweed, common thistle, hairy bittercress and sowthistle, can be exterminated quickly by regular hoeing, before they set seed.

Some perennial weeds, such as field horsetail or mare's tail, are extremely difficult to eradicate either completely or without the use of chemical weedkillers. Regular hoeing will weaken them, but the best answer is to put down anti-weed mulch.

The following steps can be followed to clear a plot.

1 Start by cutting the weeds off near to ground level using shears or a grass trimmer, as this will then allow you to gauge how much work will be needed to completely clear the plot.

2 Place all cut materials for composting, then concentrate on the remaining growth.

3 The weed roots can now be cleared either by digging out by hand or by using a weedkiller based on glyphosate on any re-growth that appears. Glyphosate breaks down on contact with the soil and therefore allows crops to be planted immediately after the weeds have died. According to the manufacturers, glyphosate is harmless to animals and the environment.

Japanese knotweed spreads by underground rhizomes and needs to be sprayed with glyphosate at six-weekly intervals to eradicate it. Japanese knotweed is not native to Britain, and, as it spreads easily from pieces of root, it must not be composted or sent for municipal composting.

4 Start by clearing a less affected part of the plot as this will provide an area that can be dug over for early planting.

If you do not wish to use chemical weedkillers, try clearing the plot one small area at a time, which you can then plant into. Clearing will be less daunting once you see an area in productive use.

The rest of the plot can be covered with black polythene or cardboard until you are ready to start clearing the next area for planting. The advantage of covering with black polythene or cardboard is that any weed growth will be suppressed by the shortage of light. You will need to place soil or bricks on the edges of the material used to prevent it blowing about in the wind. Some people recommend the use of old carpets, but these can cause problems in an allotment context. Carpets can be difficult to remove if left for a long period of time, particularly if made of artificial fibres, as the decaying carpet is not biodegradable and will fall apart when being lifted. Perennial weeds are also likely to grow through the carpet, anchoring it to the soil. Foam-backed carpet, when decaying, will separate, leaving small pieces of foam in the soil. There have also been some concerns with the potential leakage of chemicals into the soil from either the carpet dyes, or from the chemicals used to 'fix' the colour. Many councils now ban the use of carpet for these reasons.

Top tip

Allotment gardening is a long-term commitment so there is no need to do everything at once. Take your time and enjoy the process rather than tiring yourself out and turning it into a chore.

Check your soil type

It is important to know your soil type because this will make your time on the plot easier. However, first you must check the depth of the topsoil, which is the darker layer of soil containing the plant nutrients. Topsoil should ideally be a minimum depth of 46 cm (18 inches). If the topsoil is shallower, it might be advisable to construct and use raised beds. Raised beds can be made by building timber or brick edges to a suitable height and filling with soil or compost.

The following are the main types of soil.

Clay soil

Clay soil is heavy and sticky, difficult to work, but often high in nutrients. Clay soil will be improved by the addition of sand, grit and organic matter (including home-made compost). The addition of garden lime also assists in breaking down the soil particles. Avoid treading on the soil when it is wet as this will compact it. Preferably dig over in autumn to allow the winter weather to break it down. Clay soils hold water and nutrients well, but may take a bit of work to get into a condition that is easier to work with.

Chalky soil

Chalky soil is shallow, often stony but free-draining. Chalky soil is usually alkaline and will benefit from the addition of organic matter such as compost or farmyard manure.

Sandy soil

The opposite of clay soil, sandy soil is light, easy to work and free-draining, but it is liable to erosion and does not retain water or nutrients. Sandy soil is much easier to work with and to clear weeds from. However, it requires the addition of a considerable amount of bulky organic matter and therefore may take a while to improve.

Silt

Similar to sandy soil, silt has a higher level of nutrients. It benefits from the addition of organic matter to help with moisture retention.

Peaty soil

Peaty soil is high in organic matter with good moisture retention, but sometimes can be too wet. Peaty soils are usually acidic.

Loam

Loam is the ideal as it is a good mixture of clay and sand particles.

Soil testing

Once you know your soil type, you should carry out a pH test to find out if it is alkaline or acid. Soil testing kits are available from most garden centres and are supplied with instructions for use.

The pH of a soil is a measurement of whether it is acid (e.g. peaty soil) or alkaline (e.g. clay soil). Most vegetables are fairly tolerant but some, like brassicas (members of the cabbage family), are unhappy in soil that is too acid, while others, like rhubarb and radish, are acid-tolerant.

The best reading for most edible crops is between 5.5 and 7.5. A pH of 7 is a neutral soil; above 7 is alkaline and below 7 is acid. If your soil is on the acid side, apply garden lime before planting out brassicas (broccoli, cabbage, cauliflower, etc.) as they prefer the soil slightly alkaline. If the soil is alkaline, add garden compost and manure to raise the acidity levels.

Soil testing can also provide you with an indication of the levels of important nutrients, such as nitrogen, potash and phosphate, so that you can ensure these vital plant foods are available in adequate quantities in the soil. If the levels are low, you should increase them by adding plenty of organic matter or by using balanced fertilizers (which also include nitrogen). If they are high, only add nitrogen as this is lost quickly from the soil. You only need to test the soil every three to four years.

Organic and inorganic matter

Manures and fertilizers

What is the difference between a manure and a fertilizer? The dividing line is not clear, however, there are some general principles.

Manure: Manure is a term used by gardeners to describe the bulkier soil foods of organic origin such as rotted animal dung, or composted plant waste.

Fertilizer: Fertilizer is taken to be the more concentrated forms of inorganic food such as nitrogen, sulphates and phosphates.

Why do I need to add manure or fertilizers to the plot?

Growing crops remove a lot of the vital nutrients from the soil and so manure or fertilizers are needed. Even in uncultivated soil, manuring of a kind takes place by the action of worms that pull decaying leaves and other vegetation into the soil, and also by the surface decay of vegetation by many small creatures. As the vegetable grower requires a more intensive cropping than would occur naturally, this exhausts the soil of many vital plant foods more rapidly.

Every fertile soil contains enough plant food in a suitable form for immediate use by the plants, and also holds reserves of all the essential chemicals that in time will be available to the plants by the actions of the weather and soil organisms. All the gardener has to do is to supplement these natural supplies and balance them where one is in excess or is in short supply, or where a particular crop has special nutrient needs.

There is a distinction between feeding the soil and feeding the plants. Both are necessary but the first is the more important of the two. Feeding the soil means adding substances to it that will enrich it chemically for a considerable time, and will also stimulate the living organisms that form so vital a part in soil fertility and structure. Dung and compost come into this category and so do nitrogenous fertilizers applied with a 'green manure' to assist in its decay. Green manure is explained on page 21.

When plants are suffering from a chemical deficiency and the rapid feeding of plant nutrients becomes necessary, you must use chemicals that can be either accessed by the plant straight away or those that can be broken down in one or two stages. Examples of these are Epsom salts (magnesium sulphate) sprayed on to a crop as a 'foliar feed', which will immediately combat magnesium deficiency, and bonemeal, which is not soluble in water and only releases the useful nutrients after a period of disintegration in the soil.

Essential foods

There are many 'chemicals' that are essential in the soil for the growth of plants, but the four most important, which are most likely to be deficient in the soil, are nitrogen, phosphorus, potassium (potash) and calcium. Consequently, these are the chemicals that the gardener will most frequently need to supply. Magnesium runs a close fifth and is followed by sulphur, iron, boron, manganese, copper and zinc. It is usual to refer to the first five of these as major and the remainder as trace elements because they are required in smaller quantities but are equally essential to healthy plant growth.

What each food does

Nitrogen has an effect on the rate and vigour of growth and colour of foliage. When nitrogen is in short supply, plants tend to be stunted and leaves are small and pale. Add a high nitrogen fertilizer to growing crops and the rate of growth immediately increases and the leaves become large, lush and green. Nitrogen can also be found in well-rotted compost, manure or other organic material.

Phosphorus also has a considerable effect on growth, particularly on roots that grow freely when it is abundant, but are poor and stunted when it is lacking. This is one reason why fairly large doses of phosphatic fertilizers are always advised for root crops. It is important that seedlings and other young plants have sufficient phosphorus so that they can form a good root system. Phosphorus also has a marked effect on the satisfactory ripening of seeds and fruits. Phosphorus is available as superphosphate fertilizer or bonemeal.

Potash (potassium carbonate) is the main fruit-forming fertilizer. When there is insufficient potash in the soil in relation to the nitrogen present, fruits tend to be poorly coloured and lacking in flavour – faults that disappear directly when potash is added. Potatoes grown in potash-starved soil cook badly, turning black and soapy. Potash also has a striking effect on foliage. When it is deficient, the leaves, particularly of fruit trees, become scorched at the edges as much as they would by drought or excessive heat. Potash was originally derived from the refined ashes of broad-leaved trees. Potash is available as sulphate of potash.

Calcium is the element added to the soil when adding garden lime. Calcium enters into the constitution of all plants and is essential to them, but generally there is sufficient in the soil for their needs. Lime must be regarded as one of the major soil foods because of its importance to the soil itself where it breaks down clay and corrects acidity, stimulates bacterial activity and aids the freeing of other plant foods.

Magnesium is used in the formation of chlorophyll, the substance that makes leaves green. When in short supply, leaves develop purplish or brown patches between the veins and may fall prematurely. Epsom salts will rectify this. Iron in some way assists chlorophyll because plants that are short of iron develop yellow or very pale leaves. Treat iron deficiency by choosing the right soil conditions for the plant (for example, avoid growing acid-loving plants in lime soils), or by adding rotted manure or compost, or by applying an appropriate plant tonic available from garden centres.

Complete or compound fertilizers

The terms 'complete' or 'compound fertilizers' are used to describe any mixture of chemicals that provides nitrogen, phosphorus and potash in reasonable quantity, which are regarded as supplying all plant food that may be deficient in the soil. These three elements are the most likely to be in short supply so the so-called 'complete fertilizer' is the best general standby for the gardener. Commercial fertilizers indicate what percentage of each element is contained within it.

Manure

Farmyard or stable manures are ideal for use on a plot as they tend to be fairly high in nutrients. They should be well rotted and preferably stacked in a heap for a minimum of 12 months before use, or spread as a deep layer over the soil in the winter for digging in during the early spring. Poultry manure is equally good, but is stronger, contains higher levels of calcium, and needs to be well rotted before use.

Garden compost is easy to make on the plot from any waste organic matter such as weeds and unwanted produce. Garden compost is a free and renewable resource that contains good levels of nutrients.

Spent mushroom compost is a bulky waste material used as a soil structure improver. It contains lime and is good for brassicas, but regular use will raise soil pH levels.

Green manures are crops grown specifically for digging in to incorporate into the soil as a soil improver. They also help smother weeds and prevent nutrients leaching from the soil. Green manures are available in several varieties, including rye grass, mustard, crimson clover and field beans, enabling a different crop to be sown and grown throughout the year.

Choose varieties that are suitable for sowing when your soil is not needed for a growing crop. Some varieties are not winter hardy, which means that you will not have to dig them in as their roots will have done their work.

Top tip

Get together with other plotholders to enable manure to be purchased and delivered in bulk.

It has recently been discovered that some farmyard and stable manures have been contaminated with an agricultural grassland weedkiller, causing symptoms of stunted growth, cupped leaves and fern-like growth. This particularly affects potatoes, tomatoes, beans and peas.

The active ingredient that causes the problem is aminopyralid. This sticks to the grass, which is then eaten by the cattle or horses and passes through them into the manure without harming the animals.

Aminopyralid can take up to two years to break down when stored, but will break down more quickly by soil bacteria. You should therefore ask your supplier to confirm that this chemical has not been used on their animal feed. It is also advisable to spread any suspect manure on your plot and rotovate it in at least three months before planting with crops.

The UK Pesticides Safety Directorate confirms that there is no risk to human health from this product, and that produce from affected land is safe to eat.

To recap, the first things you should do when you get your allotment are as follows:

1 Remove all weeds by hoeing/shearing and applying the relevant weedkiller.
2 Examine the topsoil.
3 Check the soil pH.
4 Fertilize and enrich the soil if necessary.

Planning your plot

Crop rotation

If crops are grown in the same place year after year, yields will inevitably decrease. By adopting a crop rotation system you will help prevent soil-borne pests and diseases building up as you will not be growing the same crop on the same piece of ground each year. Crop rotation also helps to make the best use of the nutrients in the soil. Each vegetable has differing nutrient needs that would otherwise be depleted. A further benefit of crop rotation is that it helps to control weeds and maintain good soil structure.

A three-year rotation is advised, however, there are no set rules on how you should divide your plot – it will depend on what you like to eat and what you can grow.

A simple plan is as follows:

Year 1   Root vegetables: potatoes, beetroot, carrots, parsnips, turnips, etc.

Year 2   Brassicas: cabbage, cauliflower, etc.

Year 3   Legumes (beans and peas) and other fruiting crops.

Anything that doesn't naturally fit into these crop groups can be grown in any one of the three.

The following year, rotate the groups but always move them in the same direction! (See Figure 1.)

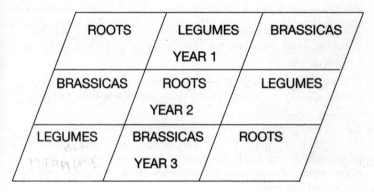

Figure 1 Crop rotation

Top tip

If, like in most allotment gardens, there are problems in following a strict crop rotation plan, don't panic. Simply ensure that crops are not grown in the same place in successive years.

It is a good idea, particularly if you are new to vegetable growing, to keep a plan of your plot and where the various crops have been planted, or are to be planted. By planning your plot you can make sure that you have sufficient space in which to plant everything you want to grow. You will also be able to plan successive crops by deciding what to replace each harvested crop with. A record of where and what has been planted also eliminates the problem of lost labels.

It is also helpful to record the dates when seeds are sown, the variety, and crops harvested, including yield, to decide which varieties are most suited to your particular plot, as this can vary from one area to another.

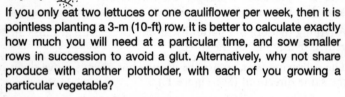

Top tip

If you only eat two lettuces or one cauliflower per week, then it is pointless planting a 3-m (10-ft) row. It is better to calculate exactly how much you will need at a particular time, and sow smaller rows in succession to avoid a glut. Alternatively, why not share produce with another plotholder, with each of you growing a particular vegetable?

Dividing the plot into separate beds is the simplest method of planning crop rotation, as this breaks cultivation down into smaller areas.

If your plot is on sloping ground, badly drained, or the soil is of a poor quality, or you have mobility problems, then raised beds might be the answer.

Raised bed gardening (see Figure 2) is a style of gardening where the soil is raised 15 cm (6 inches) or more above the surrounding soil level. As there is no need for paths between plant rows, crops can be planted closer together, thereby increasing the yield.

Raised beds can be constructed from old floorboards or gravel boards, nailed or screwed together, to whatever height is suitable for your purposes, and then filled with soil or compost. Raised beds approximately 1.2 m (4 ft) wide will allow the plot to be cultivated from either side, without the need to tread on and compact the soil. It will also be easier to construct cloches and covers for crop protection on beds this width. Bed length should be no more than 3 m (10 ft), or you will have a long walk to reach the other side, and will increase the risk of walking on the bed to get there.

Waist-high raised beds can be built for those who are less able to avoid having to bend over to tend the crop.

Raised beds dry out faster than conventional ones and hence will require regular watering and manuring.

Raised beds are also easier for children to use when gardening.

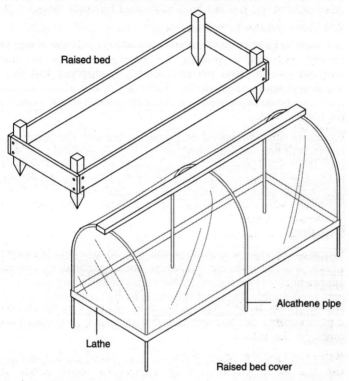

Raised bed

Alcathene pipe

Lathe

Raised bed cover

Figure 2a Raised bed **b** Raised bed cover

Top tip

In the past, old railway sleepers have been used to make raised beds. The chemicals used to preserve the wood are now considered to be hazardous to health and there are fears that they can leach out and affect growing crops. There is also a question about where sleepers come from, as it is believed many are now sourced from Eastern Europe, which raises questions as to the effect that their transportation has on the environment. Try to avoid using them if you can.

Working the soil

Soil preparation is important to ensure that seeds have a fine tilth of soil in which to germinate and send out roots. Root crops also need a soil fine enough in which to grow and expand. This is particularly significant on heavy and/or compacted soils, or where the soil has not been cultivated for some time.

Soil also needs to be free-draining, aerated, and supplied with nutrients to ensure healthy plant production. Digging or forking over the soil enables weeding by burying annual or removing perennial weeds, and allows the dug compacted soil to be weathered and broken down. Turning the soil allows organic matter to be incorporated and also exposes soil-borne insects to the birds.

The more time you spend on preparing the soil, the better your results will be. Assuming the land is already in good condition, very little cultivation might be required. A dressing of stable or farmyard manure should be applied either before digging the plot over or to the trenches during digging.

Digging

'Digging' means turning over the soil to one spade's depth, which will be suitable for most soils, particularly on old allotment plots (see Figure 3). New sites or badly neglected plots may need double digging if the soil is badly compacted and does not drain well. Double digging is also advisable in the preparation of ground where you intend to use a raised bed system.

'Double digging' involves digging a trench to two spades' depth, bringing the lowest soil to the top. As the subsoil is often infertile, such digging is not often practised and, where it is, compost or manure needs to be mixed in.

On large plots it might be easier to divide the plot in two by running a line down the centre (see Figure 4).

Start by digging a trench one spade's depth and 30–40 cm (12–15 inches) wide, and place the soil in a wheelbarrow to be taken to the end of the plot where it can be used to fill the last trench. Add a layer of manure or compost to the trench if necessary, and dig the next trench using the soil to fill the first trench. Continue turning each trench into the previous one until the first plot is completely dug over. Use the soil from the first trench to fill the last one.

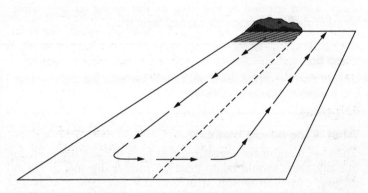

Figure 3 Digging soil

Figure 4 How to dig a wide plot

The plot will then need levelling by breaking down any clods using a rake, and then raking the soil over until a fine tilth is achieved. If digging in the autumn, leave the plot roughly dug so that the weather will break it down further and rake it over in the spring.

On light or well-worked soil, a light forking may be all that is needed. Forking is digging over the soil with a fork rather than a spade so that the soil is loosened.

If your allotment is on a new site, it might be located on old grassland: in this case ask the landlord to plough the land and rotovate it to provide conditions suitable for vegetable growing. Alternatively, the turf should be skimmed off, with a spade, in a thin layer, and put to one side. Dig a trench to one spade's depth and remove the top soil to the end of the plot. The subsoil can then be broken up with a spade or fork to one spade's depth to improve drainage. Start digging the second trench by removing the turf which can then be placed upside down on the broken up subsoil in the first trench. The second trench topsoil is then placed on top of the first trench. Continue until the whole plot has been dug over and place the first turf and topsoil into the last trench. The buried turf will eventually break down.

Planting the plot with potatoes will help to break down the soil further.

When should I dig?

Clay or heavy soils are best dug in the autumn to allow frost to break down the particles and to allow the winter rain to drain away. Light ground is best dug in the spring as any winter weathering may destroy its natural structure.

> **Top tip**
>
> Avoid treading on the soil when it is wet because this will compact it, making it difficult to cultivate.

What is the no-dig method?

There is an argument suggesting that once the plot has been dug initially, there should be no need for further digging, as annual digging can destroy soil structure, dry out lighter soils and disturb beneficial soil-inhabiting organisms. The argument goes that as most root growth takes place in the top 20 cm (8 inches) of soil, all that is required for growing is for the surface soil to be loosened and a mulching of organic matter added regularly. Worms then pull the material down into the soil, improving structure and fertility. The bed then only needs a light annual forking over to provide a fine tilth for sowing seeds into. This method is certainly suitable for use in a raised bed system.

To recap, after establishing your soil type and fertilizer needs, don't forget to do the following:

1 Plan out your plot.
2 Dig over your plot.
3 Establish a crop rotation plan.

04

tools, techniques and resources

In this chapter you will learn:
- what basic gardening tools you will need
- how to compost your green waste to improve your plot
- the essential bonfire code for safe bonfires
- how to water economically.

Tools

Initially, only a few basic tools are essential for the allotment, and these include the following.

- **Spade** – the main tool for digging and turning the soil.
- **Fork** – used for breaking down the soil and removing perennial weeds.
- **Hoe** – pushed along just below the soil surface to cut off emerging weed seedlings.
- **Standard garden rake** – used for levelling the soil and creating a fine tilth for seed sowing.
- **Hand fork and trowel** – used for planting.
- **Watering can**.

Other useful equipment and tools, which can be obtained as required, include:

- gloves
- string
- secateurs
- pruning saws
- shears and knife
- canes
- bucket
- sharpening stone or flat file
- wheelbarrow
- power tools such as a rotary cultivator.

Top tip

As you may not need a wheelbarrow or power tools all the time you could consider sharing this equipment and cost with other plotholders.

It is worthwhile investing in good quality tools as these can last a lifetime and save money in the long run. However, if you do not want to invest too much at the beginning, check out the second-hand shops, car boot sales and Internet auction sites for a bargain.

Check your tenancy agreement to see if you are allowed to have a shed or smaller containers as this can save a lot of time and effort transporting tools back and forth to your plot.

You may also need pots and seed trays. While pots and trays are fairly inexpensive, it is possible to recycle plastic food trays and tubs instead. Yoghurt pots are excellent for potting up seedlings, and plastic meat and fruit trays can be used as seed trays providing they are at least 2.5 cm (1 inch) deep. They will all need holes punched in the bottom for drainage. This can be done with a hot knitting needle or other spike, but ensure the handle is insulated to prevent getting burnt hands.

Composting

All soils benefit from the addition of organic matter, and there is no better way than to make your own compost. This is the perfect way of recycling waste garden matter, and your garden will be the better for its addition.

As most allotment waste can be composted, all that should be left for disposal by other methods is diseased or woody materials. Hedge trimmings and prunings from fruit bushes and trees can be shredded or chopped up and added to the compost. These will help to heat the heap and as a result speed up the rotting process. A domestic compost heap is unlikely to reach a sufficiently high temperature to kill plant disease, so it is best to dispose of diseased materials in your recycling bin.

The simplest method of producing compost is to pile it in a heap and leave it to nature to break it down, but putting it in a bin or container will help it to warm up and, in doing so, break down more quickly. There are various commercial compost bins available, and some local authorities also provide them at subsidized cost. A cheaper alternative is to make bins out of old wooden pallets (see Figure 5). Nailed or tied together and treated with a wood preserver they will last several years.

An allotment site will require at least 2 cubic m (70 cubic ft) of composting space, preferably split into at least two bins or heaps. When the compost in the first bin has rotted and been removed, turn the compost from the second bin into the first. This way you will always have one full bin rotting and the second being filled with garden waste.

Compost heaps need a mixture of 'green' waste, including vegetable peelings, grass clippings and other vegetation, and 'brown' waste, including leaves, cardboard, shredded paper, etc., to ensure the heap retains a reasonable amount of moisture, but does not become too wet or dry.

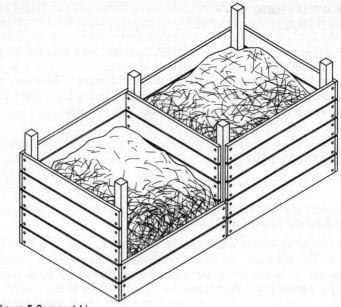

Figure 5 Compost bin

Add the materials in different alternate layers (green and brown). Covering the compost with carpet or black polythene will help to warm up the heap and enable the moisture content to be regulated.

Compost heaps need to be turned regularly to ensure that air is added because the bacterial and fungi stage, which initially breaks down the organic matter, needs oxygen. Initially, the compost heap will heat up to enable the organisms and fungi to start working. Once the bacteria and fungi have done their work and the heap cools, worms and other insects invade the heap and digest what is left.

The composting process can take from as little as six months to one year depending on many factors, including the type of materials used and the weather conditions. Do not let the compost heap dry out or become too wet as this will inhibit the breakdown process.

How will you know when your compost is ready? Compost is ready when it is dark brown, crumbly and smells of earth.

Composting 'do's'

The following can be put into your compost:

- garden waste (e.g. grass cuttings, hedge clippings, prunings, old plants and flowers and weeds)
- kitchen waste (e.g. fruit and vegetable peelings, tea bags/leaves, coffee grounds, egg shells)
- sawdust and wood ash
- cardboard
- autumn leaves (small amounts only as they can take time to rot down). If a large amount is available, put them into black bin bags or old compost bags and add them gradually as they begin to rot down. Alternatively, rot them down separately.
- shredded woody prunings
- shredded paper and newspaper
- bedding from vegetarian pets such as rabbits, guinea pigs and hamsters.

Composting 'don'ts'

The following should not be put into your compost:

- annual weeds in flower as any seeds may not degrade
- meat, fish, bread, etc. as these attract rodents
- dog/cat faeces, due to the risk of disease
- glass, plastic, metal
- glossy paper or paper with coloured ink, as these are difficult to rot
- plants infected with persistent diseases (i.e. clubroot and white rot)
- cork
- ash resulting from burning painted wood.

Top tip

On heavy soils, spread the rotted compost over the plot in autumn as this allows worms to take the compost into the soil and also makes it easier to cultivate in the spring.

What is a wormery?

Worm composting is different to conventional composting as it avoids the bacterial stage. All the work is done by compost worms (brandlings otherwise known as tiger worms) that specialize in feeding on rich organic waste.

A wormery is a plastic bin with internal dividers. Kitchen waste is placed in the top of the bin, and the worms eat it. The end product is a liquid high in nutrients that is drained off at regular intervals to be used as a fertilizer. The remaining solids can be used as a top dressing for the soil or for making potting compost.

Although less messy than a traditional compost heap, such a system may not be suitable for an allotment as a constant supply of kitchen waste is unlikely to be available and would in any case probably be best fed to hens.

Brandling worms are not found naturally in the soil, but always seem to find their way into a well-balanced compost heap.

Top tip

Brandling worms are available from specialist suppliers, but speak to other plotholders who, if they have them in their compost heap, might be willing to give you some to start your own colony. Worms can also be bought on the Internet.

Commercial compost

There are a number of proprietary composts available from garden centres, which have been specifically formulated as a growing medium. Composts are either for seed sowing, potting or general/multi-purpose.

Although plants will grow and survive in ordinary garden soil, composts have been developed to ensure a good and consistent medium with sufficient nutrients and minerals to get the seeds and plants off to a good start.

Previously, gardeners would make their own compost mix but the inexperienced gardener may be better to buy it ready-made.

Seed compost

Seed composts need to be low in nutrients as seeds themselves contain sufficient nourishment to support their early growth until the first two true leaves appear. After this stage, the seedlings will need to be potted into a more nutrient-rich mix or fed.

Commercial seed composts are made to have a fine texture and high water retention capabilities. They usually contain peat or a peat substitute such as coir, sand and sterilized loam (a rich fertile soil).

Potting compost

Potting composts can be soil-less or loam based. Although soil-less composts hold moisture, they tend to lose nutrients quickly and are more suited to plants that will be in the pot for a short time only. Potting composts can also be used for propagating cuttings. Loam-based composts provide a balanced supply of nutrients over a long period.

Both soil-less and loam-based composts drain freely, avoiding waterlogging of roots.

Multi-purpose compost

This is an all-round general purpose compost containing all the right plant nutrients, plant food, and organic matter to ensure healthy growth. It is perfect for seed sowing, potting, and use in tubs and baskets.

John Innes compost

The John Innes Horticultural Research Institute provided standardized seed and potting composts for the first time in the 1930s. John Innes composts are usually known by a number, as follows:

- John Innes No 1 – loam-based compost for potting up seedlings and young plants
- John Innes No 2 – loam-based compost for final potting of house, pot and patio plants
- John Innes No 3 – loam-based compost for final potting of hungry plants such as tomatoes
- John Innes Seed and Cuttings – loam-based compost with essential plant foods for seed sowing, rooting cuttings and pricking out.

John Innes composts are not suitable for ericaceous (acid-loving) plants like azaleas, heathers and camellias, which require a specially formulated compost. See Chapter 03 on soil types.

tools, techniques and resources

04

Top tip

Multi-purpose composts are often cheaper than specialist seed or potting composts. Good results can be equally achieved by mixing a multi-purpose compost with horticultural sand or vermiculite.

Bonfires

Bonfires have now become an unacceptable way of disposing of waste garden materials because of the toxins that are inevitably produced in the smoke. Allowing smoke to drift across a highway or creating a nuisance to neighbours by smoke, dirt and fumes is also a statutory nuisance punishable by a fine and/or imprisonment, making it more sensible to reuse this material rather than burning it. Many councils now ban bonfires on allotments to avoid any such problems.

If your council does allow bonfires, and if there is absolutely no other way to dispose of the waste, then make sure you follow this essential bonfire code.

- Only burn dry materials.
- Avoid lighting a bonfire in unsuitable weather. Smoke hangs in the air on damp still days and in the evening.
- Avoid burning when the wind will carry smoke over roads or into other people's property.
- Check the air quality and avoid burning when it is 'poor', for example, misty or damp, as the smoke will hang around and won't disperse easily.
- Never burn household rubbish, rubber or anything containing plastic, foam or paint.
- Never use old engine oil, methylated spirit or petrol to light the fire or to encourage it.
- Avoid burning at weekends and on bank holidays when people are more likely to be in their garden or to have washing out.
- **Never** leave a fire unattended or leave it to smoulder – douse it with water if necessary.
- **Remember to check for hibernating hedgehogs and sleeping pets before lighting your fire.**
- Where possible, burn your rubbish in an incinerator or container.

To recap:

1 Establish you have the right tools.
2 Get your compost heap going.
3 Make sure you have the right compost.
4 Dispose of rubbish appropriately.

Water

Treated mains water is an expensive commodity that should not be wasted. Most allotment sites are metered and it is important to find out whether you pay separately for the water you use in your rent or whether it is paid for by the association.

The use of hosepipes for watering should be avoided because they use in excess of 900 litres (200 gallons) per hour, most of which is wasted as it evaporates rather than being taken up by the plants. Moreover, if every plotholder wanted to use a hosepipe at the same time, water pressure would be compromised.

It is preferable to use a hosepipe to fill a water butt(s) that enables water to be readily available for watering the plant roots with a watering can.

Where possible, a system for saving rainwater should be set up for watering plants as this will avoid the use of treated water, and it is free.

Top tip

Avoid watering seeds in pots and trays with rainwater as algae can grow on the surface of the soil and may affect germination.

In the summer, it is better to water in early morning or in the cool of the evening rather than in the heat of the day, to avoid evaporation. Water should also be applied to the soil around the plants themselves to enable it to get directly to their roots. A good watering a couple of times a week is better than frequent light watering, since the latter encourages the plants to produce roots near the surface which will dry out more quickly.

In many areas, plants, once established, need little if any additional water. This will encourage a deep root system and help the plants get the most benefit from soil moisture.

Watering crops – dry season

Jerusalem artichoke	Never water, it encourages the formation of leaves and not tubers.
Beans, broad	Water once the pods have set.
Beans, French	Moisture at the roots is essential to produce good pods over a long period.
Beans, runner	Regular watering necessary.
Cabbage (winter)	Water by soaking the planting hole and surrounding soil prior to planting out.
Carrot	Never water, it will lower the yield.
Cauliflower	If the soil is very dry, puddle in to help them establish.
Cauliflower (summer)	Regular watering is necessary to stop the plants running to seed.
Celery	Large quantity of water is required.
Courgette, marrow	Water when fruits start to swell, then water regularly.
Cucumber	Water throughout the growing season to improve both yield and flavour.
Leek	Water thoroughly when planting, and then on a regular basis. The more water, the bigger the crop.
Lettuce	Water from sowing to harvest to produce rapid tender plants.
Onions	In a very dry season, water the ground before planting to get your sets off to a good start. Then water as required if the soil dries out.
Parsnips, swedes	No beneficial effects from watering.
Peas	Water throughout the life of the crop.
Potato	Water only when the flowers have just opened.
Spinach	Regular watering will extend the harvest.

Sweetcorn	Water when young and when the ground is dry.
Tomato (outdoor)	Regular watering will increase yield but may reduce flavour.
Turnip	In a dry year, water the bed about a month before harvesting.

Hosepipe ban

A hosepipe ban will be imposed by the local water authority when the water table drops below a certain level. Local authority allotments are not classed as private gardens and are exempt from such a ban, but it would probably be best to avoid using hosepipes during such periods or you will run the risk of annoying neighbouring gardeners to whom such bans apply.

Drought orders

These are issued by the Secretary of State for immediate enforcement by the local water authorities. They forbid the use of any but recycled water on allotment sites, whether these are private or publicly owned. Drought orders carry an unlimited fine or imprisonment for failure to comply.

Drought orders can be lifted only by the Secretary of State, and even if an area has an excessive amount of rain, the water table might not reach a sufficient level for the order to be removed.

Representations to government that growing food is an essential use of water that should not be subject to drought orders have so far been unsuccessful.

Crops that tolerate little water

Globe artichoke	Established beds do not require watering except in exceptionally dry conditions.
Jerusalem artichoke	Require watering once or twice in a dry August.
Beetroot	Too much water will increase leaf growth rather than root size. Prevent the soil from drying out.

Brussels sprout	Established plants will only require watering during exceptionally dry weather.
Carrot	The soil should not be allowed to become too dry. Watering mature carrots may cause the roots to split.
Winter cauliflower and broccoli	These should not require any watering except to establish transplants.
Chicory	After germination, chicory is left unwatered to encourage deep root growth.
Garlic	Garlic grows early in the season when moisture tends to be high.
Kale	Watering is not required after transplants have established.
Kohlrabi	The root system of kohlrabi is sufficient to draw water from a large area and therefore withstands dry conditions better than other crops.
Leek	Once the plants have established, further watering is not normally required.
Onions	Onions are deep rooted and require little watering after establishing. Watering after mid-July may delay ripening.
Parsnip	Too much watering produces leaf growth instead of root growth. Do not allow to dry out as rain after a prolonged dry spell will cause the roots to split.
Potatoes	There is usually enough water in the soil to meet the needs of potatoes.
Radish	Too much water produces leaf growth and poor roots.
Swede	Too much water produces large but poor-flavoured crops. Avoid the soil drying out.
Sweetcorn	Once established, sweetcorn needs little water until the tassels have formed.

Crops that tolerate wet weather

Few crops are suited to wet conditions. The following table shows those that are more tolerant than others, but they should not be allowed to become waterlogged.

Celery	Watering improves the size and quality of the plants. Regular watering is necessary to avoid the sticks becoming stringy.
Courgette, marrow, pumpkin, squash	Marrows and courgettes require a lot of water at flowering time and in dry conditions.
Rhubarb	Rhubarb has a high water requirement particularly during summer.
Spinach	Frequent watering is required to ensure good quality, rapid growth and maximum yield.

05

what to grow

In this chapter you will learn:
- which crops you should grow
- how to buy seeds
- how to grow and cook your vegetable crops
- about herbs for flavour
- about fruit varieties.

Which crops?

Grow crops that you, your family (and friends) enjoy eating before becoming too adventurous. Keep it simple to start with by growing just a few varieties rather than trying to grow everything and possibly failing with some crops. Easy crops to begin with are early potatoes, spinach, lettuce, onions grown from sets, runner beans, sweetcorn, beetroot and other salad crops. For winter you might try purple-sprouting broccoli and kale.

Most vegetable growers raise plants from seed, but garden centres now have increasing ranges of vegetable plants available, including tomatoes, cucumber, lettuce, cabbage, aubergine and sweet peppers. If you only require one or two plants of any particular variety this might be a more economical way of obtaining them.

Seeds

All seed varieties must now be registered on a national list that includes the standards the seed must achieve and meet. Each seed variety is required to have a 'maintainer' who is responsible for ensuring the variety remains true to type under laboratory conditions, including purity, the percentage of seeds germinating, size of crop yield, etc.

Seeds require optimum growing conditions, such as temperature, light levels and moisture, to ensure good germination. To ensure satisfactory results, it is important that the growing instructions on the seed packet are followed. Growing conditions may vary between the north and the south of the UK, and it might be necessary to sow seeds slightly later the further north your plot. Once a grower has gained more experience and knows the local conditions, it will be easier to experiment with the timing of seed sowing.

Most seed companies now include details of either the number of seeds in the packet or the number of plants that can be grown under average conditions. If a seed packet says there are 200 seeds, this does not mean that all 200 will germinate. Similarly, if a seed packet shows that the contents are sufficient to produce 50 plants then there will be more seeds in the packet to ensure that the required percentage germination takes place. When looking at value for money, you will need to take this into consideration.

Seeds grown indoors or under glass need to be hardened off (acclimatized to the outside conditions) before planting out. This is done by bringing the plants out into the open or opening the lid of the cold frame during the day and returning them at night for several days before planting out.

Top tip

While there are many different varieties of each type of vegetable, not all may be suitable for your soil conditions or location. What grows well in the warmer southern counties may not be suitable for northern climes. When in doubt, ask other plotholders which varieties they find grow best in the locality.

What is meant by F1 hybrid seed?

'F1 hybrid seed' is a term used for selective cross-breeding of varieties to produce a new uniform variety with specific or desirable and consistent characteristics, for example, vigour, colour, disease resistance or hardiness. Two varieties are cross-pollinated through controlled hand pollination until the desired result is achieved.

The disadvantages are that the resultant crop from F1 hybrid seed tends to mature at the same time, which might result in a glut, and seed saved from an F1 hybrid will not grow true to type and should be avoided.

Due to the method of production, F1 hybrid seed is more expensive than open-pollinated varieties, but consistency is guaranteed.

Sowing seeds

To sow seeds, follow these steps:

1 Push a stick or cane into each end of a row and tie a length of string between them.
2 Use the corner of a hoe or stick to draw a shallow trench along the line of the string.
3 A trench 5 cm (2 inches) deep for large seeds and a shallow one 2.5 cm (1 inch) deep for small seeds is usually suitable, but check the seed packet for specific instructions.
4 Dribble water along the bottom of the trench if the soil is dry.

5 Sprinkle seeds evenly along the trench. Do this by taking a pinch of seeds and releasing them a few at a time, or by holding the open seed packet just above the trench and gently tapping it. Large seeds are best sown individually.

6 Fill the trench very lightly by raking the surplus soil back into it.

7 Firm the soil by tapping the row with the head of a rake.

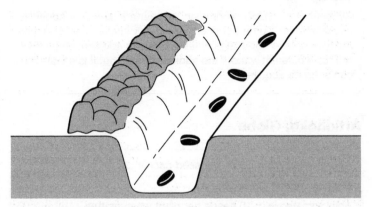

Figure 6 Seed trench with individually sown seeds

Which varieties are best for flavour?

Like wine, vegetable flavours are very much a matter of individual taste. What one person considers sweet, another might find too sickly. In other words, everyone has their own favourite.

Flavour is affected by various factors, including growing conditions. Weather, moisture and soil nutrients will all contribute to the speed and size at which a crop matures, and a faster growing crop often seems to have more flavour. Moreover, open-pollinated varieties often have a better flavour than hand-pollinated ones.

It has to be remembered that once a vegetable has been picked or dug up it is severed from any further nutrients and water uptake, and will deteriorate over a period of time. It is always best to eat produce that has been freshly picked and is young. The methods of harvesting, storage and cooking can also affect flavour.

Vegetable varieties

The following advice is for guidance only and you must look at the information on the seed packet for more specific growing instructions for each variety of vegetable.

> **Top tip**
>
> Although it is usually recommended that a little salt is added to cooking water, current concern about salt intake is encouraging many people to cook vegetables without its addition. Vegetables will taste different without the addition of salt, but it is a taste that can soon be acquired.

Artichoke, Globe

Approximate plant count per seed packet: 30

Popular variety: Green Globe

Approximate yield: 10 heads per plant when mature

Pests: Aphid, slugs

Artichokes have a productive life of four years and take approximately one and a half years between planting and cutting the heads. They take up a lot of space, are susceptible to cold and frost, and require winter mulching. However, they are worth a try if you want something different and have the plot space available. They require a good fertile soil in a sheltered sunny spot, with plenty of organic matter to retain moisture and provide nutrients.

Sow the seeds under glass in a greenhouse or cold frame from February to March or directly into a nursery bed in April for planting out the following spring. Plant the seeds 1 m (3 ft) apart.

Plants may produce a few small heads in the first year, but these should be cut off and discarded to enable a strong plant to develop.

Alternatively, globe artichoke plants (offsets) can be purchased for planting out immediately.

Harvest when the head is large but before the flower opens. A second crop will develop from side shoots and these can be cut off when about the size of an egg. They are usually sliced and fried.

Cooking

Cut off the stalk and remove the outer layer of scales; rinse and drain. Boil in salted water for 30–40 minutes. To eat, remove each scale and dip the base in melted butter, vinaigrette or hollandaise sauce and scrape off the fleshy base between the teeth. When the scales are removed, eat the heart. Alternatively, remove all scales, scrape away the hairs to expose the heart and boil for 15–20 minutes.

Artichoke, Jerusalem

Approximate plant count: 20 tubers

Approximate yield: 1.5 kg (3 lb) per plant

Pests: Slugs

Jerusalem artichokes are grown from tubers and produce a further 1.5–2.5 kg (3–5 lb) of tubers per plant approximately one year from planting. They can be served as a substitute for potatoes.

Plant the tubers 15 cm (6 inches) deep at 40-cm (16-inch) intervals, in rows 1 m (3 ft) apart, and earth up when the stems are 30 cm (12 inches) tall. They will grow in any soil but do well in well-manured clay soil.

Plants may need support, particularly in windy areas. A post at each end of the row with strings tied either side will provide this.

In autumn, once the leaves have turned brown, cut the stems to 30 cm (12 inches). Lift the tubers from October to early spring. If the ground is likely to become frozen, the tubers can be lifted and be stored in a frost-free place.

At the end of the season, save some of the tubers for planting the following year.

Cooking

Scrub the tubers immediately after lifting, and boil in their skins in salted water with a teaspoonful of vinegar for 20–25 minutes. Serve with melted butter.

Asparagus

Approximate plant count: 10 crowns

Popular varieties: Pacific, Guelph Millennium

Approximate yield: 20 spears per mature crown

Pests: Asparagus beetle, slugs

Asparagus is a long-term crop that has a life expectancy of up to 20 years and will take up a lot of space for that period of time. It is grown from one-year-old plants (crowns), which take a further two years before producing a reasonable crop. It can be difficult to cultivate and will rot if it is too wet.

Plant the crowns on ridges 20 cm (8 inches) deep at 60-cm (2-ft) intervals, in rows 1 m (3 ft) apart. They require a deep, weed-free, well-drained but moisture-retentive soil with a pH above 6.5.

Cut the spears just below the surface from the second year after planting, when they have reached 13 cm (5 inches) high. Stop cutting in early to mid-June to allow the spears to develop and put energy back into the crowns for the following year's crop.

Cooking

Cut off the woody parts from the base of the stems and, using a sharp knife, peel away the skin below the tips. Wash and tie in bundles with string, with the tips together. Place upright in a pan of boiling salted water with the tips above the surface. Cover and cook for 10–15 minutes.

Aubergine

Approximate plant count per seed packet: 30

Popular varieties: Long Purple, Snowy

Author's choice: Long Purple

Approximate yield: 5 fruits

Pests: Whitefly, aphid, red spider mite

Aubergines are best grown under glass in a greenhouse or cold frame or in a sunny sheltered spot. They require a well-drained and fertile soil. They can also be grown in growbags.

Sow seeds individually in pots or modular trays indoors from January to March at a 45-cm (18-inch) distance apart. Continue to re-pot as necessary. Remove the growing point when the plant has reached 30 cm (12 inches) to encourage side shoots to develop. Restrict the plants to five fruits. Water regularly and feed when fruits have formed.

Harvest when the fruit is 13–15cm (5–6 inches) long while the fruit is still shiny, about 20 weeks after sowing.

Cooking

Trim both ends and slice or dice. Coat with seasoned flour (with salt, pepper and herbs added) and fry in butter or olive oil. Alternatively, brush slices with butter or oil and grill or bake.

Stuffing: Cut in half lengthways and scrape out the pulp leaving a 2.5-cm (1-inch) thick shell. Make a savoury mixture including mince, onions and the pulp, and pile into the shells and bake at 160°C (325°F, Gas mark 3) for 20–30 minutes.

Recipe books often suggest that aubergines should be sliced and soaked in salted water to remove the bitterness, but in modern varieties the bitterness has been bred out of the plants.

Beans

Beans are very nutritious, being high in protein and a good source of calcium and iron. Home-grown beans are far superior to those available in many shops as they are picked and eaten when fresh. All beans can be sown directly into the soil or sown in pots or trays under glass and planted out after all chances of frost are passed. Seeds grown under glass have the advantage of being planted out as plants, thereby avoiding gaps in the rows.

Broad beans

Approximate plant count per seed packet: 40

Popular varieties: Aquadulce Claudia for autumn sowing, Jubilee Hysor, The Sutton (dwarf variety)

Author's choice: Aquadulce Claudia

Approximate yield: 400 g (14 oz) per plant

Pests: Blackfly

An easy crop to grow, with some varieties that can be sown in the autumn for overwintering, as well as spring sowing. Early sowings produce a better yield. A very tasty crop, but one of low yield for the space required.

Sow seeds or plant in double rows 5 cm (2 inches) deep, 20–25 cm (8–10 inches) apart in March or early autumn in deeply worked soil, or in February under cloches. Sow a few extra seeds to fill any gaps. Alternatively, sow under glass in early spring and plant out when the plant is 10 cm (4 inches) high. Sow seeds every two to three weeks from March to May to ensure a crop from late spring to early summer. Tall varieties might need support.

Broad beans are best picked young. Harvest once the bean is showing in the pod, approximately 26 weeks after sowing, but before the skins mature and become tough. Pods can also be harvested when young and eaten whole.

Cooking

Top and tail young tender beans and cook whole in their pods. Slice diagonally and eat. Mature beans should be removed from their pods. Drop into boiling salted water and cook for 10 minutes.

Broad beans are particularly tasty served with fried or boiled bacon.

French beans

Approximate plant count per seed packet: 65–125, depending on variety

Popular varieties: Borlotto, Blue Lake. For a novelty, try Yard Long

Author's choice: Blue Lake

Approximate yield: 300 g (11 oz)

Various types of French beans are available, including climbing, dwarf, flat, pencil-podded and coloured. Regular picking is required to ensure flowering for a continuing crop. French beans are grown either for eating as pods or for producing beans for drying for winter casseroles.

Sow seeds directly into the soil at 10-cm (4-inch) intervals from May, or under cover from mid-February for an early crop.

Seeds can also be sown indoors from March for planting out once all risk of frost has passed. They require warm moist soil for best results.

Climbing varieties need to be supported on canes but there are dwarf varieties available that are planted at 30-cm (12-inch) intervals.

Harvest when the pods are 10 cm (4 inches) long and a pencil thickness, approximately ten weeks after sowing. Try to pick before the bean seeds start to swell. Dried beans can be saved at the end of the season.

Cooking

Top and tail (remove the stalk and bottom end) and put into a pan of lightly salted boiling water and cook for 5–10 minutes.

Runner and kidney beans

Approximate plant count per seed packet: 35

Popular varieties: Enorma, Painted Lady, Desiree, Hestia (dwarf)

Author's choice: Polestar, Painted Lady

Approximate yield: 1 kg (2 lb) per plant

Britain's favourite, but often sold when they are past their best. Dwarf and climbing varieties are available. Regular picking is required to ensure a continuing crop.

Sow seeds in rows 5 cm (2 inches) deep and 20 cm (8 inches) apart with 60 cm (2 ft) between rows from early May. Earlier sowings may be made in individual pots or trays under glass or in a cold frame and planted out after all risk of frost has passed. Pinch out the growing tip when the plants reach the top of the canes to encourage the formation of side shoots.

Mature plants require a lot of moisture and therefore need a deeply worked soil with the addition of large amounts of compost to retain the moisture. In windy areas, choose a sheltered site.

Runner beans require supporting on canes, and can also be grown in 'wigwam' circles if space is at a premium (see Figure 7).

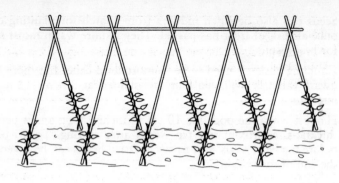

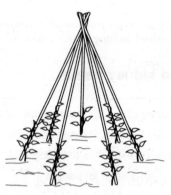

Figure 7a Bean frame **b** Bean wigwam

Harvest when the pods are 15–20 cm (6–8 inches), approximately 14 weeks after sowing.

Cooking

Top and tail, and slice diagonally. Place in lightly salted boiling water for 5–10 minutes.

Top tip

Runner beans need regular watering in dry weather conditions because they like a cool damp root run, but they do not like badly drained soil. To retain moisture, dig a trench and add manure, shredded newspaper or cardboard, water it and backfill with soil. The beans can then be sown or planted in the filled trenches.

Top tip

All beans produce nitrogen nodules on their roots. At the end of the season, cut the plants off at ground level leaving the roots to rot and the nitrogen nodules to enrich the soil.

Beet, Leaf

Approximate plant count per seed packet: 200; coloured varieties – 100

Popular varieties: Perpetual Spinach, Swiss Chard, Rainbow Chard

Approximate yield: 3.5 kg (7 lb) per 3-m (10-ft) row

Pests: Slugs

Swiss chard and spinach beet are fairly easy to grow and will overwinter. Use and cook like spinach.

Sow seeds directly into the growing site 2 cm (¾ inch) deep in rows 35–40 cm (14–16 inches) apart, from May to March. Gradually thin to 20 cm (8 inches) apart.

Harvest outer leaves when they are suitable for use in the kitchen, approximately 12 weeks after sowing. Pick regularly, avoiding the middle foliage and disturbance to the roots.

Cooking

Use the foliage as a spinach substitute and cook the stalks separately in the same way as asparagus spears. Steam the fleshy leafstalks for 20 minutes or chop them into sections and boil for 15 minutes.

Beetroot

Approximate plant count per seed packet: 250

Popular varieties: Boltardy, Detroit, Cylindra (long stump rooted)

Author's choice: Boltardy and Cylindra

Approximate yield: Globe varieties 4.5 kg (10 lb) and long varieties 7.5 kg (16½ lb) per 3-m (10-ft) row

Home-grown beetroot can be used all year round, either picked fresh during the summer or from roots stored over winter. It is available in globe and long stump rooted varieties, and yellow and white flesh varieties.

Sow seeds thinly in shallow drills 2 cm (¾ inch) deep. Thin the seedlings to 10–15 cm (4–6 inches) apart. Sow short rows at weekly intervals to ensure continuous cropping. Beetroots grow in most soil conditions but are best in well-drained and humus-rich soil.

Harvest when the beetroots are large enough for use, 10–15 weeks after sowing. Globe varieties should be picked before they reach 10 cm (4 inches) in diameter. Long varieties are lifted in October for storage over winter in dry peat or sand.

Beetroot can also be stored wrapped in newspaper and kept in a dry frost-free shed.

Cooking

Tear off the stalks 3–5 cm (1–2 inches) above the base. Wash carefully but avoid damaging the skin to prevent the beetroot 'bleeding', which will cause loss of colour during the cooking.

Boil in water for 1–2 hours, depending on size. After boiling, remove the skin and eat hot or leave to cool to serve in salads. Traditionally, cold beetroot has been pickled in vinegar to preserve it, but it is better cooked and eaten fresh because of its own delightful sweet flavour.

Broccoli

Approximate plant count per seed packet: 200–500, depending on variety; F1 hybrid – 50

Popular varieties: Purple Sprouting, White Sprouting. For a novelty, try Romanesco, which produces lime green heads.

Author's choice: Purple Sprouting and Nine Star Perennial

Approximate yield: 700 g (25 oz) per plant

The name is often used to describe both calabrese and sprouting broccoli. Broccoli contains folic acid, another B vitamin, and vitamins C and E. Calabrese produces green heads in the autumn, and broccoli has both purple and white sprouting varieties that are ready in the spring. Broccoli is used on a 'cut-and-come-again' basis.

Sow seeds from April to July, depending on variety, 1 cm (½ inch) deep in fertile soil. As seedlings appear, thin them to 7 cm (3 inches) apart. When they are 10–15 cm (4–6 inches) tall, transplant to the growing site at 45-cm (18-inch) intervals.

Harvest when the central spear is well formed but has not flowered, approximately 44 weeks after sowing. Side shoots then develop, producing smaller heads that are cut off as they mature.

Cooking

Wash thoroughly and drain. Remove any large leaves, peel any tough stalks and cook in lightly salted boiling water for 10 minutes. Many people now prefer broccoli to be steamed for 20–25 minutes.

Brussels sprouts

Approximate plants per seed packet: Standard varieties – 200–300; F1 hybrid – 60

Popular varieties: Bedford, Evesham Special; F1 varieties – Cascade, Maximus

Author's choice: Bedford and Cascade

Approximate yield: 1 kg (2 lb) per plant

Brussels sprouts contain vitamin E. A range of varieties is available to ensure a crop from autumn until March. They are best eaten freshly picked as tight 'buttons'.

Sow the seeds indoors in pots or trays from February and plant out in May at 45–60 cm (18–24 inch) intervals. Alternatively, sow outdoors in a seed bed from March to April and transplant to the growing site from May to June. Prepare the bed well in advance to allow the soil to settle as sprouts prefer a firm soil.

Pick the sprouts before they start to open, starting at the bottom of the stem, when they are 3–5 cm (1–2 inches) in size, approximately 30 weeks after sowing.

Cook and eat sprouts as soon as possible after picking.

Cooking

Wash and trim off any damaged outer leaves and stalk and boil in lightly salted water for 10 minutes. Do not allow sprouts to overcook and become soggy as they will lose their flavour.

Cabbage

Approximate plants per seed packet: Standard varieties – 300–400; F1 hybrid – 70

Popular varieties: Spring – Durham Early, Flower of Spring; Summer – Greyhound, Primo; Winter – January King, Tundra F1, Red Drumhead

Author's choice: Durham Early, Greyhound and January King

Approximate yield: 0.5–1.5 kg (1–3 lb) per plant

Pests: Cabbage root fly, cabbage white butterfly, aphid

Cabbage is a good source of vitamins A, C, B1, B2, B3, D and K. It is also high in potassium and calcium, but loses half of these minerals during cooking. There are spring, summer, and winter cabbage varieties, of which many types are available. Cabbage is possibly one of the most versatile vegetables available as it can be eaten both raw and cooked. Sufficient varieties are available to produce a crop all year round.

Sow spring varieties thinly from July to September in a prepared seed bed in shallow drills. Thin seedlings to 5 cm (2 inches) apart and transplant to the growing site when 10–15 cm (4–6 inches) tall, planting at 35–40 cm (14–16 inches) apart.

Sow summer and autumn varieties in February under cover, or in late March to May directly into a seed bed. Thin seedlings to 5 cm (2 inches) and transplant to the growing site when 10–15 cm tall (4–6 inches).

Sow winter varieties thinly in a nursery bed in April and May and transplant to the growing site in July, 45 cm (18 inches) apart.

Spring cabbage thinnings can be used as spring greens, but other cabbages are harvested once the hearts are firm, 20–35 weeks after sowing depending on variety.

Cooking

Prepare just before cooking. Remove coarse outer leaves, cut the cabbage into quarters, and remove the hard centre core. Wash thoroughly and cook either shredded or in wedges. Cook in lightly salted water for 5–8 minutes. Serve tossed with butter and seasoning.

Top tip

When harvesting cabbages, leave a few leaves on the stalks and cut a cross on the top of the stalk. This will result in a further crop of small cabbages.

Capsicum (sweet and chilli peppers)

Approximate plant count per seed packet: sweet varieties – 70; chilli varieties – 35; F1 hybrid – 7

Popular varieties: Sweet – Sweet Spanish mixed. Also available in individual colours of green, red or yellow. Chilli – Apache

Author's choice: Sweet Spanish mixed

Approximate yield: 6–10 fruits per plant

Pests: Red spider mite, aphid

Capsicum peppers contain vitamins A, C and K. Varieties include large sweet peppers and chilli peppers with varying degrees of heat. Peppers are best suited to greenhouse conditions, but can be grown outside in a sunny sheltered position, particularly if covered with a cloche.

Sow sweet pepper seeds indoors from March to April in pots. When the first flower shows, transplant to growbags or large plots. When 30 cm (12 inches) tall, remove the growing tip to encourage side shoots.

Harvest as required when the peppers are large enough for your purposes, or leave them until they change colour from green to red, yellow or orange, depending on variety, approximately 18 weeks after sowing.

Cooking

For stuffed peppers, cut around the stalk and remove the seeds and inner pith. Parboil for 10 minutes, drain and fill with a savoury meat or vegetable filling. Add a little stock to moisten, and bake at 180°C (350°F, Gas mark 4) for 25–30 minutes.

Carrot

Approximate plant count per seed packet: 750

Popular varieties: Amsterdam Forcing, James Scarlet, Early Nantes for an early crop, Autumn King, Flyaway F1

Author's choice: James Scarlet and Sugarsnax

Approximate yield: Early varieties 3.5 kg (8 lb), maincrop 4.5 kg (10 lb) per 3-m (10-ft) row

Pests: Carrot root fly

Carrots are high in beta-carotene, which the body converts into vitamin A. They are a very popular crop, available in short-rooted, intermediate-rooted and long-rooted varieties.

Short-rooted varieties mature quickly and are the earliest to be sown. As they mature quickly, they can also be sown as a late crop in some regions of the country. Intermediate varieties are generally sown later as a maincrop for winter use. Long-rooted varieties are mainly grown for the show bench in specially prepared soil. They are not really suited to general garden use unless your soil is deep, rich and light.

Sow seeds thinly under cloches in February, or directly into the ground between March and July, in rows 30 cm (12 inches) apart. Pull out alternate roots when small, and use whole as baby carrots. Aim for roots 5 cm (2 inches) apart for the maincrop. For continuous cropping, sow short rows fortnightly.

A light, well-drained soil with plenty of organic matter will provide the best results. Stony or heavy soil will cause the carrots to fork or become misshapen.

Small carrots can be harvested or left until they reach a suitable size for your use, approximately 12–16 weeks from sowing.

Cooking

Carrot skins are thin, so peeling young carrots should not be necessary. Scrub clean and remove the root and leaves. Peel older carrots if necessary. Cut larger carrots into quarters, rings, cubes or sticks and place in sufficient lightly salted water to just cover them and boil for 10–20 minutes.

Cauliflower

Approximate plant count per seed packet: 50–150, depending on variety

Popular varieties: Summer – All Year Round, Candid Charm; Autumn/Winter – Wainfleet, Berlot F1. Purple-headed varieties are now available.

Author's choice: All Year Round and Candid Charm

Approximate yield: 0.5–1 kg (1–2 lb) per plant

Pests: Slugs

Cauliflowers can be difficult to grow as they require a rich, deep and firm soil, but the flavour makes them worth trying. There are sufficient summer, autumn and winter varieties available to provide a crop for most of the year.

Think about when you want to harvest your crop, and choose the relevant seed variety.

Sow seeds of summer and autumn varieties directly into the soil from February to May. Thin to 5 cm (2 inches) apart and transplant to a permanent site from May to June. Sow seeds of autumn and winter varieties from April to June and transplant to a permanent site after approximately six weeks. Sow in a well-prepared bed with lots of organic matter incorporated. The soil needs to be firm, so prepare well in advance to allow the soil to settle.

Harvest once the heads have formed and are of a sufficient size for your use, approximately after 20 weeks for summer and autumn varieties, and after 45 weeks for winter varieties.

Cooking

Divide into florets, wash thoroughly, and boil in lightly salted water for 12–15 minutes. Small cauliflowers can be cooked whole.

Do not overcook as the cauliflower should be slightly crisp (al dente) and not soggy.

Serve as a plain vegetable or with white or cheese sauce.

Celeriac

Approximate plant count per seed packet: 600

Popular varieties: Each seed company seems to have its own varieties.

Author's choice: Prinz

Approximate yield: 3.5 kg (8 lb) per 3-m (10-ft) row

Pests: Carrot root fly, celery fly, slugs

Easy to grow, but celeriac requires sowing early to ensure good size roots. The roots have a distinct celery flavour. Use grated in salads or as a roasted or boiled vegetable in soups and stews.

Sow under glass in February and March and in seed trays or modules or outside from March to April. Plant out in May, in any fertile soil, in rows 30–35 cm (12–14 inches) apart each way. During September, any shoots that are growing from the side should be cut off and a little soil drawn around the bulb to keep it white.

Harvest from October, approximately 30 weeks after sowing.

Cooking

Wash, slice and peel, then cut into cubes or matchstick strips. Boil in lightly salted water, to which lemon juice has been added, for 25–30 minutes.

Serve with melted butter. Celeriac can also be shredded and added to salads.

Celery

Approximate plant count per seed packet: 300

Popular varieties: Golden self-blanching, Giant Red (trenching)

Author's choice: Golden self-blanching, Aurora

Approximate yield: 7–10 plants per 3-m (10-ft) row

Pests: Celery fly, slugs

Celery is a popular salad vegetable grown for its crisp sweet stalks. Traditionally, it was grown in trenches and 'earthed up' as the crop grew, to blanch the stems. There are now self-blanching varieties available that are easier to grow, have a milder flavour, but are not frost-hardy.

Sow the seeds under glass in February in seed trays or modules for an early crop, or in March and April for a maincrop. Prick out into individual pots as soon as they can be handled. Harden off (acclimatize) plants before transplanting into the growing site in late May or June, in blocks for self-blanching types with 30 cm (12 inches) spacing each way. Traditional varieties should be planted in a trench 40 cm (16 inches) wide and 30 cm (12 inches) deep, prepared the previous autumn. Space plants 35–45 cm (14–18 inches) apart, filling in the trench as the plant grows.

Celery requires a water-retentive soil with plenty of organic matter incorporated.

Harvest self-blanching varieties as required approximately 25 weeks after sowing and before November. Trench varieties should be harvested approximately 20 weeks after sowing.

Cooking

Outer stalks can be sliced and added to stews and soups, or they can be stir-fried.

Chicory

Approximate plant count per seed packet: 500 forcing types; 400 leaf types

Popular varieties: Forcing – Brussels Witloof; Leaf – Palla Rossa

Author's choice: Witloof

Approximate yield: 2.75 kg (6 lb) per 3-m (10-ft) row

Pests: Cutworms, slugs, wireworms

This crop is used for crisp winter salads, but as chicory can be slightly bitter it is not to everyone's taste. Two forms of chicory are available: one producing lettuce-like leaves, the other for forcing to produce blanched 'chicons'.

Forcing types. Sow seeds 1 cm (½ inch) deep in rows 30 cm (12 inches) apart in May or early June; thin seedlings to 20 cm (8 inches) apart. Between October and December the roots should be lifted. Trim off the leaves, which can be used in salads, to leave about 2 cm (¾ inch) above the neck of the root. Store in a frost-free shed until required. Shorten the root length to 20 cm (8 inches) and plant four to five roots close together in a large pot. Place an inverted pot on top, covering any holes to exclude the light to help to reduce the bitterness. Place in a warm environment, and chicons should be ready in three to four weeks.

Leaf types. Sow seeds thinly in the growing site 1 cm (½ inch) deep between April and July or in seed trays or modules. Thin or transplant to 25 cm (10 inches) between plants. Sow seeds in August or September under polythene for winter heads. Leaves can be picked regularly after about four weeks or left until mature and then the whole head can be harvested. Leave the stump in the ground and you will get a small re-growth of young leaves.

Chicory requires a deeply worked soil to enable the taproot to develop.

Harvest the forcing varieties when the chicons are 15 cm (6 inches) high, approximately four weeks after forcing.

Harvest non-forcing varieties in late autumn and store in a cool shed.

Cooking

Add chicons to lightly salted boiling water and simmer for 10 minutes. Drain and serve with cheese or tomato sauce. Alternatively, serve crisp and raw in salads.

Courgette

Approximate plants per seed packet: Standard varieties – 15; F1 hybrid – 10

Popular varieties: All Green Bush, Zucchini. Yellow-skinned varieties are also available.

Author's choice: Zucchini and Jemmer (yellow variety)

Approximate yield: 15 courgettes per plant

Courgettes are a member of the marrow family. They should be picked young because continuous cropping is necessary to keep the plants in production.

Sow single seeds, pointed end facing downward, in pots or modules under glass in April or direct into the growing site when all risk of frost has passed. Cover with a cloche or jam jar to encourage germination. Allow 90 cm (3 ft) each way around the plants.

Courgettes require a free-draining soil and a constant supply of water. This can be achieved by planting on a mound of organic matter covered with soil.

Harvest when the courgettes reach a suitable size, approximately 12 weeks after sowing. If left to grow larger and form marrows, production will be affected.

Cooking
Best lightly fried in butter or olive oil and eaten while they still have a bite (al dente) rather than cooking them longer and letting them go soggy.

Cucumber

Approximate plants per seed packet: Standard varieties – 16–30, but varies depending on variety; F1 hybrid – 4

Popular varieties: Glasshouse – Passandra F1; Outdoor – Telegraph Improved, Burpless Tasty Green

Author's choice: La Diva and Burpless

Approximate yield: 20 per plant indoor, 10 per plant outdoor

Pests: Red spider mite, slugs, snails

This salad vegetable has varieties available for indoor or outdoor production. The long types available in the shops are grown in heated greenhouses, but outdoor varieties can be equally tasty.

Glasshouse varieties. Sow seeds on their edge in individual pots or modules from late February to late April under glass at 20°C (70°F). Plant in a greenhouse or in growbags in late March or April. Train the stem up wires or canes and remove the growing tip when it reaches the roof. The plants require a humid atmosphere.

Outdoor varieties. Sow seeds direct in the growing site from mid-May, 30 cm (12 inches) deep and 45 cm (18 inches) apart. Alternatively, sow seeds earlier under cloches or glass in pots or modules. Cucumbers need water-retentive soil with plenty of organic matter, but this should not be allowed to become waterlogged. This can be achieved by forming mounds and planting on them.

Harvest when the plants have reached a suitable size, approximately 12 weeks after sowing. If left to grow large and turn yellow, further cropping will be reduced or stop altogether.

Endive

Approximate plants per seed packet: 200

Popular varieties: Seed companies appear to have their own varieties

Author's choice: Pancalieri

Approximate yield: 10–15 heads per 3-m (10-ft) row

Pests: Aphid, slugs

Endive is a continental salad vegetable, growing in popularity in Britain. It is slightly more bitter than lettuce, but a tasty addition to any salad.

Sow seeds thinly from March to September in rows 1 cm (½ inch) deep. Thin seedlings to an eventual spacing of 25–30 cm (10–12 inches) apart.

Harvest when the leaves have turned creamy white, approximately ten weeks after sowing.

Kale (or Borecole)

Approximate plant count per seed packet: Up to 350, depending on variety

Popular varieties: Dwarf Green Curled, Redbor F1

Author's choice: Dwarf Green Curled

Approximate yield: 1 kg (2 lb) per plant

Pests: Resistant to many of the major problems, kale is susceptible to aphid, whitefly and cabbage white butterfly

An ideal vegetable for winter use, kale is very hardy and produces tender leaves that should be picked when young.

Sow seeds thinly in a nursery bed 1 cm (½ inch) deep in April or May. Thin to 10 cm (4 inches) apart and transfer to the final site in July, planting 45 cm (18 inches) apart.

Kale will tolerate poorer soil conditions than cabbage, but better soils will produce better results. The soil must be firm to prevent the plants from blowing over in the wind.

Harvest young leaves from November, approximately 30 weeks after sowing. Remove yellowing or old leaves that will cause the development of side shoots which can be gathered the following spring.

Cooking

Wash thoroughly and add to a small amount of slightly salted boiling water. Cover and simmer on a medium heat for 8–10 minutes.

Kohlrabi

Approximate plants per seed packet: 100–400, depending on variety

Popular varieties: Green Delicacy, Purple Delicacy

Author's choice: Purple Delicacy

Approximate yield: 20 globes per 3-m (10-ft) row

Pests: Aphid and birds

Not very popular in Britain, kohlrabi is an alternative to turnip, with a similar but milder flavour. It grows better than turnips in hot and dry weather.

Sow seeds 1 cm (½ inch) deep in rows 30 cm (12 inches) apart in late February or March once the soil has warmed, and then every couple of weeks for a continuous supply. Thin the seedlings to 20 cm (8 inches) apart as soon as possible.

Harvest when the swollen stem is about 6 cm (2 inches) in diameter, approximately ten weeks after sowing.

Cooking

Trim the leaves off the globe and scrub. Small globes can be cooked whole, while larger globes can be peeled, sliced or diced. Boil in slightly salted water for 30–60 minutes depending on size.

Serve with melted butter. Boiled Kohlrabi can also be mashed with butter or sour cream.

Leek

Approximate plant count per seed packet: 100–300, depending on variety

Popular variety: Musselburgh

Author's choice: Giant Winter

Approximate yield: 4.5 kg (10 lb) per 3-m (10-ft) row

Pests: Leek moth

Leek is a tasty winter vegetable that is in the ground for quite a long time. Easy to grow, winter hardy varieties are available, enabling cropping from October to May. The roots can help to break up heavy soils.

Sow the seed thinly in a nursery bed in March and April, 1 cm (½ inch) deep in rows 15 cm (6 inches) apart. Thin the seedlings to 4 cm (1½ inches) apart. When the seedlings are the thickness of a pencil and about 20 cm (8 inches) tall, they are ready for transplanting. Make a series of holes 15 cm (6 inches) deep in rows 30 cm (12 inches) apart with 15 cm (6 inches) between holes. Lift the young leeks and trim a little off both the roots and leaves and drop one plant into each hole (see Figure 8). Do not fill the hole, but water regularly to gradually bring soil into the hole. Gradually earth up to produce white stems that should be complete by October. Winter varieties can be left in the ground as they are very hardy.

A deeply worked soil rich in organic matter will produce better leeks.

Harvest as soon as the leeks reach a reasonable size, approximately 40 weeks after sowing.

Figure 8 Planting leeks

Cooking

Cut off the top of the leaves but do not remove all of the green tissue, and remove any coarse outer leaves. Wash carefully under a cold tap to remove any soil from the leaves. Leeks can be left whole if small, cut in half lengthways, or sliced into thick rings. Boil for 10 minutes and drain thoroughly.

Best served with a white sauce or as a soup.

Top tip

Leeks can be sown in deep trays rather than in nursery beds, but they require regular watering and feeding.

Lettuce

Approximate plant count per seed packet: 500–1,000, depending on variety

Popular varieties: Butterhead varieties (soft leaves) – Buttercrunch, Tom Thumb; Crisp/iceberg varieties – Trocadero, Webbs Wonderful; Cos varieties – Little Gem; Salad leaves (cut and come again) – Salad Bowl

Author's choice: Salad Bowl, Little Gem and Webbs Wonderful

Approximate yield: 10–20 heads per 3-m (10-ft) row

Pests: Slugs and snails, cutworms and aphid

Lettuce is the salad special, available in many different varieties and colours with both indoor and outdoor types for spring, summer, autumn and winter harvest. Lettuce contains vitamin B2.

Although fairly simple to grow, a lettuce crop can be decimated by pests. Lettuces can also run to seed fairly quickly after maturity, particularly in hot weather, so it is advisable to sow at regular intervals to ensure a continuing crop.

Small lettuces can be spaced at 15–20 cm (6–8 inches) intervals; crisp lettuces, such as iceberg types, at 30–35 cm (12–14 inches) spacing, in rows 30 cm (12 inches) apart. Sow seed from February under glass, followed by outdoor sowings until late autumn. Overwintering varieties must be protected by cloches or planted in the greenhouse from an autumn sowing. Lettuces prefer a free-draining, moisture-retentive soil. Lettuce seed will go dormant if sown in hot weather so find a cool place to sow the seed.

Harvest 'heading' varieties, such as Butternut and Webbs Wonderful as soon as they have hearted up, approximately ten weeks after sowing, or use the thinnings as and when required.

Marrow

Approximate plants per seed packet: 15

Popular variety: Long Green Bush

Author's choice: Long Green Bush and Vegetable Spaghetti

Approximate yield: 4 marrows per plant

Pests: Slugs, snails and mice

See also 'Courgette' and 'Squash and pumpkin' sections. With marrow, these are all members of the same family of plants, but with different uses. Most varieties can be used to produce both courgettes and marrows. Marrows can be cut and stored for winter use.

If you have limited space, the varieties grown as courgettes are much more prolific. Allow your courgettes to grow a little bigger as this saves space.

Raising and growing requirements are the same as for courgettes.

Harvest the plants as soon as they are large enough for your use, approximately 12 weeks after sowing.

Cooking

Peel, seed and cut into cubes for boiling, or cut into thick rings for stuffing. Marrows may also be cut in half lengthways, with the seeds removed, for stuffing. Boil for 10 minutes or, for stuffed marrow, bake in an oven at 190°C (375°F, Gas mark 5) for 45–60 minutes, or, for marrow rings, cover with foil and bake for 25–30 minutes.

'Vegetable Spaghetti Marrow' is a recent addition. When cooked, the flesh inside is scooped out and resembles spaghetti. Harvest when about 20 cm (8 inches) long, cook whole, scoop out the flesh inside and add ground pepper and butter. Vegetable marrows have a trailing habit.

Onion and shallot

Approximate plants per seed packet: Maincrop – 200–300; spring onions (salad use) 350–600

Popular varieties: Bulb onions – Bedford Champion, Red Baron; Spring onions – White Lisbon; Onion sets – Red Baron, Sturon, Stuttgart Giant, Turbo; Shallot – Golden Gourmet

Author's choice: Sturon and Red Baron; Golden Gourmet shallots

Approximate yield: 3.5 kg (8 lb) per 3-m (10-ft) row

Pests: Onion fly

Very popular vegetables for the allotment gardener, onions and shallots can be grown from seed or from sets. Sets, which are immature bulbs, are probably the easiest for the new plotholder to grow as a decent crop is practically guaranteed.

Spring onions and pickling onions are grown from seed. Onions tend to be grown for storage and winter use, but overwintering 'Japanese' varieties are available from seed for summer use.

Sow seeds directly into the growing site in shallow drills 2 cm (¾ inch) deep with 25–30 cm (10–12 inches) between rows for bulb onions and 10 cm (4 inches) between rows for salad crops. Thin bulb onions gradually to 10 cm (4 inches) between plants. Salad onions do not need thinning.

Seeds can be sown in modules under glass in January or February, sowing six to eight seeds per module. Harden off (acclimatize) and plant out in March or April. 'Japanese' varieties should not be sown before mid-August and are thinned in the spring. Onion and shallot sets are planted out in their growing positions from early April.

A fertile well-drained soil with a pH of 6.5 or above is ideal.

Harvest when large enough for your use or when the foliage has died down, approximately 20 weeks after planting sets.

Cooking

Trim the roots and neck and remove any dry outer leaves. Onions and shallots can be left whole, sliced, chopped or diced. They are excellent as an accompaniment for soups, stews, casseroles and sauces, and can also be used raw in salads. Fry slowly in order for the onions or shallots to soften before browning.

Parsnip

Approximate plant count per seed packet: 600

Popular varieties: Avonresister, Gladiator, Tender and True

Author's choice: Hamburg Parsley (I have difficulty growing parsnips on my plot – see 'Top tip' opposite.)

Approximate yield: 3.5 kg (8 lb) per 3-m (10-ft) row

Parsnips are winter hardy vegetables, but they take a long time to reach maturity.

Sow seeds thinly from February to April in drills 1 cm (½ inch) deep with 30 cm (12 inches) between rows. Thin to 15 cm (6 inches) apart. Roots can be left in the ground and harvested as required.

A deeply cultivated and stone-less soil is ideal. The incorporation of manure or compost will improve yield. Use fresh seed every year for best results.

Harvest when the foliage begins to die down as required.

Cooking

Cut off the tops and roots, and peel. Cut in quarters. Boil in lightly salted water for 10–12 minutes. Alternatively, roast parboiled parsnips for 5 minutes, drain well and place in a roasting tin with oil. Roast near the top of the oven at 210°C (425°F, Gas mark 7) for 40 minutes, turning once, or roast them with a joint of meat. Boiled parsnips can be creamed with other vegetables or cooked as chips.

Serve boiled parsnips tossed in butter.

> **Top tip**
>
> If you have difficulty growing parsnips, try growing Hamburg Parsley instead. The leaves may be used, but it is grown for its parsnip-like roots.

Pea

> Approximate plants per seed packet: 200–300
>
> Popular varieties: Early varieties – Early Onward, Feltham First, Kelvedon Wonder; Maincrop – Alderman, Greenshaft, Onward; Mangetout – Oregon Sugar Pod, Sugar Snap
>
> Author's choice: Alderman and Sugar Snap
>
> Approximate yield: 4.5 kg (10 lb) per 3-m (10-ft) row
>
> Pests: Pea moth, mice

Peas picked fresh from the garden are far tastier than the frozen ones available from the supermarket. Peas are available as early varieties and as maincrop. Some varieties can be sown in the autumn for an early May crop.

The yield can be small for the amount of space the crop takes up, but peas are well worth growing for the fresh pea taste. Mangetout peas may represent better value for space, as the whole pod is eaten before the peas swell.

To get the best flavour, peas should be picked and eaten young.

The usual method of sowing is to make a drill 12–15 cm (5–6 inches) wide and 4–5 cm (1½–2 inches) deep in a moisture-retentive soil, and to sow the seeds 5 cm (2 inches) apart. Water the row and then cover with soil. Taller varieties will require support.

Autumn varieties. Sow from October to November for a May crop.

First early varieties. Sow from mid-March to mid April.

Maincrop varieties. Sow from March to May. These are suitable for successional sowing.

Autumn crop. Sow a 'first early' variety from June to July.

Mangetout and petit pois. Sow in April and May after the soil has warmed up.

Harvest when the pods are well filled but there is a little air space between each pea, approximately 15 weeks after sowing. Mangetout varieties should be harvested before the peas swell.

Top tip

The best way to test whether peas are ready is to pick a pod and eat the peas, but beware as this can become addictive!

Cooking

Shell fresh peas and boil gently for 15–20 minutes in lightly salted water with a sprig of mint. Mangetout and sugar snap peas are cooked whole.

Potato

> Approximate plant count per 2-kg packet: 20 tubers
>
> Popular varieties: First Early – Accent, Arran Pilot, Lady Christl; Second Early – Estima, Kestrel, Maris Peer, Nadine; Maincrop – Cara, Desiree, King Edward, Sante; Salad – Anya, Charlotte, Nicola, Pink Fir Apple
>
> Author's choice: Lady Christl, Pink Fir Apple and Cara
>
> Approximate yield: Early varieties – 5.5 kg (12 lb) per 3-m (10-ft) row; Maincrop – 9 kg (20 lb) per 3-m (10-ft) row
>
> Pests: Slugs, wireworm

The potato is one of the most versatile vegetables available and is very simple to grow. Buy certified seed potatoes, which are guaranteed to be disease-free, rather than saving ones bought for eating from the supermarket.

Potatoes are available as earlies (new potatoes), second early and maincrop. There are also varieties that are perfect for salad use.

A 3-kg (7-lb) bag of seed potatoes is sufficient to plant a 10–12 m (30–36 ft) row.

Upon receiving the seed potatoes, unpack them and put them on trays in an airy and frost-free place to enable them to sprout before planting out. This is known as 'chitting'.

First Early. Plant seed potatoes in late March 10 cm (4 inches) deep at 30-cm (12-inch) intervals in rows 60–70 cm (24–28 inches) apart.

Second Early. Plant seed potatoes from early to mid-April 10 cm (4 inches) deep at 30–40 cm (12–16 inch) intervals in rows 70–5 cm (28–30 inches) apart.

Maincrop. Plant seed potatoes from mid- to late April 10 cm (4 inches) deep at 40–5 cm (16–18 inch) intervals in rows 70–5 cm (28–30 inches) apart.

Salad Potatoes. Plant out as for First Early.

A deeply dug, well-manured soil is best. With all potatoes, earth up (ridge) the rows two or three times to prevent green tubers (see Figure 9).

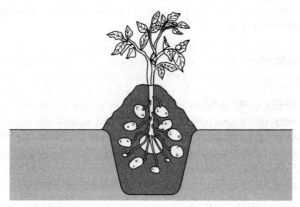

Figure 9 Earthing potatoes

Harvest after the plants have flowered, approximately 16 weeks after planting for early varieties. Maincrop varieties are harvested after the tops have died down, approximately 22 weeks after planting.

Cooking

New potatoes only need washing, lightly scraping and washing again before boiling, or they can be boiled in their skins and peeled before serving. For old potatoes (where the skin has dried), wash and peel and cut into chunks for boiling. Cook for 15–20 minutes, but as varieties often cook at different rates, test the potatoes after 15 minutes with a sharp knife or carving fork. If the knife goes into the potato without resistance, it is cooked. Avoid over-boiling, which will turn the potatoes into an inedible mush.

Boiled potatoes can be eaten as cooked or mashed and creamed with milk and butter.

For fried potatoes, boil until they are almost cooked then cut them into slices or bite-size chunks and fry until crisp and golden brown.

For chips, peel the potatoes and cut them into 2-cm (¾-inch) slices, then cut the slices into 2-cm (¾-inch) strips. Wash and thoroughly dry them before placing in a saucepan or chip pan of hot oil, and cook until golden brown. Be careful when making chips as chip pans can be a major cause of house fires. Never leave the pan unattended, and if you have to leave the room, turn off the heat and remove the pan from the burner.

For roast potatoes, parboil for 5 minutes, drain well and place in a roasting tin with oil. Roast near the top of the oven at 210°C (425°F, Gas mark 7) for 40 minutes, turning once.

Jacket potatoes only require scrubbing, pricking and placing near the top of the oven. Bake at 200°C (400°F, Gas mark 6) for 60 minutes. When cooked, cut open at the top and add butter, or another topping of your choice such as cheese, tuna mayonnaise or baked beans.

Radish

Approximate plant count per seed packet: 300–500

Popular varieties: Summer varieties – Cherry Belle, French Breakfast, White Icicle; Winter varieties – Black Spanish Long, China Rose

Author's choice: French Breakfast

Approximate yield: Summer varieties – 2 kg (4½ lb) per 3-m (10-ft) row; Winter varieties – 4.5 kg (10 lb) per 3-m (10-ft) row

Pests: Slugs

Radish is one of the easiest and quickest of vegetables to grow. Both summer and winter varieties are available. Radishes are best sown thinly in short rows at weekly intervals.

Summer varieties. Sow 1 cm (½ inch) deep in rows 15 cm (6 inches) apart in a rich well-drained soil from March to late September to ensure a constant supply. If sown too thickly and not thinned, radishes will run straight to seed.

Winter varieties. Sow from July onwards.

Mooli varieties (Japanese type). Sow from June to July to harvest in August/September.

Harvest when the radishes are large enough for your use, approximately five weeks after sowing.

Spinach

Approximate plant count per seed packet: 170

Popular varieties: Each seed company has its own varieties

Approximate yield: 2.5–4.5 kg (5–10 lb) per 3-m (10-ft) row

Spinach contains vitamin A and folic acid as well as vitamins E and K. Spinach is not as high in iron as first believed, due to a decimal place error in the original research. Leaves can either be picked young and used in salads or cooked. Summer and winter varieties are available. Summer varieties can be prone to bolting in prolonged dry weather. Regular picking is required to ensure a continuing crop.

Summer varieties. Sow every few weeks from March to August, 2 cm (¾ inch) deep in rows 30 cm (12 inches) apart, for a constant supply. Thin as soon as possible to 15-cm (6-inch) intervals.

Winter varieties. Sow during August and September, 2 cm (¾ inch) deep in rows 30 cm (12 inches) apart, for a spring harvest. Thin as soon as possible to 15-cm (6-inch) intervals.

Spinach prefers a free-draining but water-retentive alkaline soil.

Harvest the outer leaves as soon as they have reached a reasonable size and are still young and tender, approximately 12 weeks after sowing. Pick continually to encourage new growth.

Cooking

Wash leaves thoroughly to remove soil and dirt and place into a saucepan without adding any extra water. Sprinkle on a little salt; cover and cook for 10 minutes, shaking the pan occasionally. Once cooked, drain thoroughly before serving.

Squash and pumpkin

Approximate plant count per seed packet: 10

Popular varieties: Squashes – Butternut Squash, Sweet Dumpling, Turks Turban; Pumpkins – Hundredweight and Jack O Lantern

Author's choice: Butternut Squash and Sweet Dumpling

Approximate yield: Squash – 1.5–2 kg (3–4 lb) per plant; Pumpkin – up to 10 kg (22 lb) per plant

Squash and pumpkin are available in several different varieties. They are a good source of vitamin A.

Growing and sowing is the same as for courgettes, but planting distances will vary according to the variety grown.

Squashes and pumpkins prefer a soil with plenty of organic matter incorporated.

Allow the fruits to mature on the plants, but remove before there is any frost and store in a cool place.

Cooking

Wash and cut into bite-size pieces, peel and remove seeds and pith. Boil for 20–30 minutes in slightly salted water.

Alternatively, steam for 35–40 minutes. To roast, parboil for 5 minutes, drain well and place in a roasting tin with oil. Roast near the top of the oven at 210°C (425°F, Gas mark 7) for 40 minutes, turning once, or roast around a joint of meat.

Swede

Approximate plant count per seed packet: 700

Popular variety: Marian

Author's choice: Marian

Approximate yield: 13 kg (30 lb) per 3-m (10-ft) row

This is a hardy winter vegetable that is easy to grow. It has a milder and sweeter flavour than turnip.

Sow seeds thinly 2 cm (¾ inch) deep in rows 40 cm (16 inches) apart in May and June. Thin gradually until 25-cm (10-inch) intervals are achieved.

Swedes will tolerate any soil as long as the pH is not too low.

Harvest the roots as soon as they are big enough for use, approximately 22 weeks after sowing.

Cooking

Trim the stalk and roots and peel. Cut into 2–3 cm (1 inch) cubes and boil in slightly salted water for 30–40 minutes. Swede can be mashed with butter or used in stews and casseroles.

Sweetcorn

Approximate plant count per seed packet: 40

Popular varieties: Kelvedon Glory, Sweet Nugget

Author's choice: Sweet Nugget

Approximate yield: 1 or 2 cobs per plant

Sweetcorn requires a good summer for the best production. Picked and eaten fresh, the flavour is far better than shop-bought ones. Sweetcorn can be frozen fresh and used in the winter.

For best results, sow under cover in modules or pots in April.

However, sowing can be made outside in late May and June. Plant out in blocks spaced 30 cm (12 inches) apart each way. Regular watering is essential once the cobs start to form.

Sweetcorn requires good light, plenty of water and protection from north and east winds.

Harvest after the tassels have turned brown, approximately 14 weeks after sowing. Carefully peel away the leaves to reveal a small section of seeds. Press a couple of seeds with your thumb and if these are plump, soft and yellow, the cobs are ready for picking. Either use immediately or freeze for later use.

Cooking

Put the cobs into a pan of unsalted boiling water for 5–8 minutes. Drain and serve with a knob of butter.

For barbeques, wrap in buttered foil and place in the ashes for 10 minutes.

Sweetcorn kernels, frozen on the cob, can be stripped off with a knife while still frozen and then boiled for 5 minutes.

Tomato

Approximate plant count per seed packet: Standard varieties – 50; F1 hybrid – 10

Popular varieties: Outdoor varieties – Ailsa Craig, Alicante, Moneymaker; Cherry/salad type – Gardeners Delight, Sunbell, Sweet Million; Plum varieties – Roma, San Marzano; Beefsteak varieties – Big Boy, Marmande; Indoor varieties – Shirley F1, Vanessa F1

Author's choice: Vanessa F1 and Gardeners Delight

Approximate yield: Greenhouse crops – 3.5 kg (8 lb) per plant; Outdoor varieties – 2 kg (5 lb) per plant

Pests: Whitefly and red spider mite in greenhouse crops

Tomatoes are available for both greenhouse and outdoor production. Home-grown tomatoes seem to have a far better flavour than those bought in the shops.

Many different varieties of tomato are available for the amateur gardener to grow. There is a range of colours, shapes and sizes, from the small salad varieties, through plum varieties for cooking, and to large beefsteak varieties for slicing and stuffing.

Sow seeds in trays 5 cm (2 inches) apart under glass in January or February for glasshouse crops, or in March and April for outdoor crops. Once two true leaves have formed, transplant into individual pots.

In the greenhouse, plant either directly into soil or growbags, three per bag. For outdoor crops, harden off (acclimatize) the plants before planting out 45 cm (18 inches) apart, in rows 75 cm (30 inches) apart, in a well-drained but moisture-retentive soil. Stake the plants for support. Water regularly because irregular watering will cause the fruit to split and possibly cause blossom end rot.

Harvest once the fruits are ripe and fully coloured, approximately 20 weeks after sowing.

Cooking

Tomatoes can be cut in half and grilled or fried, or filled with a savoury filling and baked at 180°C (350°F, Gas mark 4) for 15 minutes. Tomatoes can also be added to sauces, casseroles, stews and salads.

Turnip

Approximate plant count per seed packet: 500–900

Popular varieties: Golden Ball, Milan Purple Top, Snowball

Author's choice: Snowball

Approximate yield: 3–4.5 kg (6–10 lb) per 3-m (10-ft) row

Turnips are quick growing root vegetables used mainly in casseroles and stews, but can also be grated raw in salad. Tender when young.

Sow the seed in shallow drills 1 cm (½ inch) deep with 20–30 cm (8–12 inches) between rows from February to April. Thin the seedlings as soon as possible to 10–15 cm (4–6 inches) apart.

Harvest as soon as the turnips are large enough to use, approximately ten weeks after sowing.

Cooking

Wash and trim the stalk and root and peel. Small turnips can be cooked whole or larger ones cut into chunks and boiled for 30 minutes in lightly salted water.

Top tip

Gardening books often suggest planting seed two or three to a pot or station and discarding the weaker seedlings. This is a waste of seed and money as the weaker seedling will soon catch up. There can also be a problem if the stronger seedling is eaten by slugs or snails or succumbs to disease. It might make more sense to sow one seed per pot or station, plus one or two extra pots to cover non-germination.

Top tip

An allotment is often short on space, and if you only eat one or two vegetables of a particular variety in a week, sowing a whole row is not economical unless you wish to share the surplus produce with friends and neighbours. As many seed varieties can be sown in trays, modules or pots, you can sow just the right amount to produce what you need on a fortnightly basis. Plants can then be potted, and re-potted, into larger pots until space on the plot is available. Make sure the pots are watered and fed regularly and do not let the plants become pot-bound.

Herbs

Herbs add flavour to cooked dishes and salads. They can also be added to vinegars and oils to give a distinctive flavour.

Herbs are annual, perennial or biennial, and can be planted in their own beds, in pots and containers, or dotted in small clumps.

Plant count per seed packet: 60–500, depending on variety.

Sow annuals and perennials directly into their growing position in spring. Perennials should be sown in spring or early summer, but can be bought as plants.

Popular varieties

Balm, Lemon. This has a similar habit to mint as it can be very invasive and is best grown in pots. Use in cooked dishes, salads and for herbal tea.

Basil. There are several varieties available with their own distinctive aroma and taste. Use in salads or stir-fries.

Chervil. Gives an aniseed flavour for mild flavoured dishes. Chervil can also be used as an alternative garnish to parsley.

Chives. There is a mild onion flavour to both leaves and flowers. Use in salads, omelettes and scrambled eggs or as a garnish.

Comfrey. The leaves are used to make fertilizer – the herb is high in potash.

Coriander. This is used in Asian and Middle Eastern dishes.

Dill. The seeds are used in pickles and sauces. Dill is also used in fish dishes.

Fennel, Bronze or Green. The leaves have an aniseed flavour and are used in pickles and cooking.

Marjoram. A member of the oregano family, marjoram is good added to tomato salad.

Mint. Many varieties are available. Green mint is traditionally used for mint sauce or mint tea. Mint is very invasive and best grown in pots.

Oregano. This is used in Mediterranean cooking, in tomato-based pasta sauces and in pizza toppings.

Parsley. Use in stuffing or mix with breadcrumbs and use as a topping or coating. Parsley is also used as a garnish.

Rosemary. Used to flavour roast lamb, pork and grilled fish. Rosemary can also be used in stuffing.

Sage. Sprinkle torn leaves over tomato salad or use in stuffing.

Thyme. Many varieties of thyme are available, including lemon scented. Used in a host of dishes, including marinades, stews and as a stuffing.

Storing herbs

Drying. The object of drying herbs is to remove the water content as quickly as possible while still retaining the essential oils. Herbs need to be dried in a warm, dark, dry and well-ventilated place. Always dry herbs separately to avoid the scent transferring to other herbs.

Dry places can include an airing cupboard, in the oven at a low temperature with the door ajar, or a plate-warming compartment.

When drying in an airing cupboard, place the herbs in a single layer on trays covered with muslin.

If drying in an oven, place the herbs on brown paper with holes punched in it, and check regularly to ensure that the herbs are not overheating.

When drying seeds, the ripe seed heads can be placed in paper bags and hung up to allow the seeds to fall into the bag as they mature. Artificial heat is not necessary, but seeds should be completely dry before being stored.

Freezing. Freezing herbs retains the flavour, colour and nutritional value. Put the herbs in a plastic bag, either singly or mixed, label and place in a container to prevent damage. The herbs can then be added to the cooking as required.

Fruit varieties

Landlords often include a clause in the tenancy agreement to prohibit the growing of crops that take more than 12 months to mature, without their approval or at all. As an allotment garden is defined in law as an area for growing vegetable *or* fruit crops, such a clause would seem to be unenforceable, as all fruit crops would be included.

If your agreement includes such a clause, ask the landlord for an explanation as to why this is required.

Soft, bush and cane fruit

Blackberry

Popular varieties: Loch Ness, Oregon Thornless

Approximate yield: Thornless varieties – up to 4 kg (9 lb) per plant

Blackberries are often considered the 'thug' of soft fruit because of the hedgerow bramble that is rampant, particularly on vacant and derelict plots. However, recent cultivars, specifically the thornless varieties, are more manageable, especially if trained on trellis, fences or frames.

Thornless varieties require less space and can be planted 2–3 m (6–10 ft) apart.

Blueberry

Popular varieties: Brigitta, Earliblue

Approximate yield: 2–5 kg (4–11 lb) per plant

Blueberries require an acid and organic rich soil and are possibly best grown in a large pot or container. They are available in early, mid- and late season varieties.

Plants need netting to prevent loss of fruit to birds.

Currant

Popular varieties: Blackcurrant – Ben Connan, Ben Lomond, Ben Nevis; Redcurrant – Rovada; Whitecurrant – Blanka

Approximate yield: 10 kg (22 lb) per plant

Black, red and white varieties are available. Currants freeze well and can be used for jam and pies. Redcurrants are high in pectin and can be added to strawberries to thicken strawberry jam.

Space plants 1.5 m (5 ft) apart.

Plants need netting as birds love them.

Gooseberry

Popular varieties: Invicta, Hinnonmaki Red

Approximate yield: 2.5–5 kg (5–11 lb) per plant

Usually used for culinary purposes, gooseberries are suitable for stewing, pies and jam; there are dessert varieties available.

Space plants 1.5 m (5 ft) apart.

Loganberry

Popular variety: Thornless

Approximate yield: Thornless variety – 5 kg plus (11 lb plus) per plant

A hybrid cross between a blackberry and raspberry, loganberries are excellent for culinary use and eating fresh.

Space plants 2.5 m (8 ft) apart.

Loganberries are now available in a thornless variety; cultivate as for blackberries.

Raspberry

Popular variety: Glen Moy

Approximate yield: 1 kg (2 lb) per 1-m (3-ft) row

The second most popular fruit in the UK, raspberries are available in summer and autumn fruiting varieties. This fruit freezes well.

Raspberries need more work than other cane fruit because they need strong supports and bird protection. They prefer a slightly acid soil. They also dislike rain, which can cause the fruit to rot and shortens the fruiting period.

Space plants 45 cm (18 inches) apart in rows 2 m (6 ft) apart.

Rhubarb

Popular varieties: Timperly Early, Champagne

Approximate yield: 2.5 kg (5 lb) per plant

Rhubarb is really a vegetable that is used as a dessert. It can be grown from seed but is best bought as crowns.

Space plants 1 m (3 ft) apart.

Strawberry

Popular varieties: Cambridge Favourite, Royal Sovereign

Approximate yield: 750 g (1.5 lb) per plant

Britain's favourite summer fruit, strawberries are best eaten freshly picked. Birds also love them, so they will need netting.

Strawberries can be grown in the ground or in pots, tubs and hanging baskets.

Early, mid- and late season varieties are available, allowing cropping from June to late autumn.

Space plants 45 cm (18 inches) apart.

Top fruit (fruit trees)

As a tenant is legally required to ensure that a plot does not deteriorate, there is a reasonable argument that planting fruit trees on 'standard' rootstocks might render the plot as unsuitable where the trees become overgrown and their roots cover the majority of the plot. It is probably better to grow fruit trees that have been grafted onto dwarfing rootstocks, such as for apples, or that have been trained as espalier, fan, cordon or ballerina as the growth is restricted and the roots will only affect a small area of the plot (see Figure 10). An outgoing plotholder would be responsible for the removal of any plants not required by the incoming tenant.

Plant bare-rooted trees (sold without any soil) from November to March. Container-grown trees can be planted at any time of the year.

Trees grafted onto dwarfing rootstocks will still require annual pruning to maintain the shape and size.

Almost all fruit trees are propagated by grafting a bud or shoot from one tree onto a root of another to produce a plant with specific characteristics. The rootstock is different from the fruiting part.

There are a number of advantages to propagating by this method, one of which is to control the vigour and final size of the tree. The specific rootstocks used are often given a number or name by which they are known.

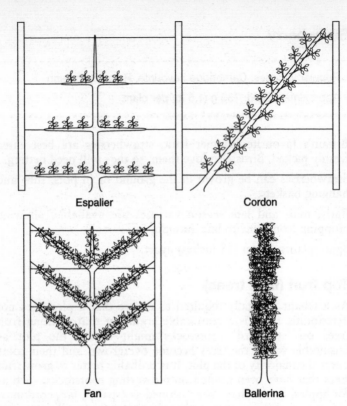

Espalier

Cordon

Fan

Ballerina

Figure 10 Four types of trained tree

Top tip

The current thinking on planting trees is to dig a square hole rather than a round hole, as the roots find it easier to penetrate the adjoining soil.

Apple

Popular varieties: Dessert – Braeburn, Cox's (choose a self-fertile clone), Egremont Russet, Red Falstaff (a good pollinating variety); Cooking – Bramley Seedling; Dessert/cooking – Crispin

Approximate yield: M27 – 6–12 kg (12–24 lb) per tree; M9 – 17–22 kg (34–40 lb) per tree; M26 – 32–7 kg (64–74 lb) per tree; MM106 – 45–55 kg (90–110 lb) per tree

Apples are available in both dessert (eating) and culinary (cooking) varieties. Different varieties are available, which are harvested at different times from late summer to mid-autumn.

Rootstocks available

M27. The smallest tree, growing to 1.5–1.8 m (4–6 ft).

M9. Growing 2–3 m (6–10 ft).

M26. Growing 3–4 m (10–12 ft).

MM106. Growing 4–5 m (12–15 ft). This is the most commonly used rootstock.

Most apples require a different variety to pollinate them as they tend not to be self-fertile, and need to be planted with at least one other compatible variety from the same group. Apple varieties are normally sold with details as to which varieties will pollinate them.

Top tip

Avoid buying 'Family' apple trees that have three different varieties grafted on, unless space is at a premium, as the most vigorous variety will always grow stronger and take over.

Cherry

Popular varieties: Stella, Sweetheart, Morello (cooking variety)

Approximate yield: 9–14 kg (20–35 lb)

Cherries are naturally vigorous, but can be grown as bush trees or fan trained. Fan trained is probably the most suitable for an allotment because it controls its vigour. A fan-trained cherry will reach 2.5 m (8 ft) high by 5 m (15 ft) wide.

Gisela 5 dwarfing rootstocks are now available.

Cherries need to be frost-free during flowering and therefore may need protection if frost is threatened. Sweet varieties need a sheltered site in full sun. Cooking varieties are less fussy.

Look for self-fertile varieties, otherwise a second cultivar from the same pollinating group that flowers at the same time will be required.

Pears

Popular varieties: Concord, Conference

Approximate yield: Between 26–60 kg (60–120 lb), with smaller yields from trained trees

Pears are grown on a more limited range of quince rootstocks, producing trees 3–6 m (10–20 ft) (half standard).

Quince C rootstock is semi-dwarfing, growing to 2.5–3.6 m (9–11 ft).

Plum

Popular varieties: Czar, Victoria (which can be eaten fresh and also used for cooking or jam making). If you only have space for one plum tree, then Victoria is the one.

Approximate yield: 13.5 kg (30 lb)

Plums are one of the easiest tree fruit to grow. However, as they flower early in the season, they are prone to frost damage and consequently cropping can be disappointing. Grow in a sunny spot for best results.

Plums need a moisture retentive, but free-draining soil. Light soils which dry easily must be enriched with humus.

Available on semi-dwarfing rootstocks, growing up to 3 m (10 ft). While there is no true dwarfing rootstock for plums, Pixy is semi-dwarfing, growing 2.4–3.6 m (8–11 ft).

The plum family also includes greengages and damsons. Damsons are excellent for jam making (and home-made wine).

06

allotment buildings and other structures

In this chapter you will learn:

- about the benefit of having a shed
- how to extend your growing season
- how to protect your crops
- how to keep your plot safe.

Allotments are defined as an agricultural use of land and so buildings are exempt from some requirements like planning permission, particularly if they can be considered temporary and not permanent, and in many cases you do not need to have planning permission in order to erect a shed, greenhouse or polytunnel. However, your landlord may need to give you permission first, and he or she may also wish to restrict the type and sizes of buildings erected on their land.

You should always bear in mind that you, as the plotholder, will be responsible for the removal or disposal of any structures erected if and when you give up the plot.

Sheds

Probably the most useful building you can have on an allotment is a shed in which to store your tools and other gardening equipment. Otherwise, you will have to carry all your tools from home each time you visit the plot.

The National Society of Allotment and Leisure Gardeners Ltd recommends that a shed up to 12 sq m (120 sq ft) should be sufficient for allotment use, and the society feels that landowners should automatically permit such size of buildings. This is not to say that a larger shed would not be justified in certain circumstances, but anything larger requires specific consent from the landowner.

It is in the interest of the plotholder, and the site in general, that sheds are treated to protect the wood from deterioration, and maintained in a good condition at all times. An unsightly or dangerous structure is unlikely to be tolerated either by the landlord or neighbours.

Sheds need to be fairly strong and capable of being secured, and it is advisable to chain tools and equipment inside the shed to make theft more difficult. Burglar alarms are now available for use in garden sheds and these are recommended as a deterrent. However, do not leave anything in the shed that cannot be replaced or that you cannot afford to lose.

Every shed should have guttering, connected to water butts, so that rainwater can be saved for use on the plot.

Greenhouses and polytunnels

Providing protection from the weather extends the growing season because it enables crops to be started earlier with quicker germination and cropping over a longer period. Crops such as tomatoes, peppers, aubergines and melons do better with protection, and winter lettuces and French beans can be grown earlier if covered.

The National Society of Allotment and Leisure Gardeners Ltd recommends that a greenhouse up to 15 sq m (150 sq ft) and a polytunnel up to 30 sq m (300 sq ft) should be sufficient for an allotment.

Greenhouses

Glass or rigid plastic can be used in the construction of a greenhouse. Glass is better because controlling the temperature is easier and it gives better light levels. However, the disadvantages are that it is fairly expensive, needs fixing to a firm base, and that so much glass is a temptation to vandals. Plastic, though cheaper, is less durable than glass.

Greenhouses need either a concrete foundation on which to fix the base, which will certainly require the written consent of the landlord, or the base needs to be secured by the use of ground anchors.

As with sheds, guttering should be connected to water butts to save rainwater for use on the plot.

There is a variety of ready-made greenhouses available from garden centres and on the Internet.

Polytunnels

Walk-in polytunnels are the cheapest choice for crop protection. UVI (ultraviolet inhibited) polythene is stretched over tubular hoops and usually held in place by burying the edges in trenches in the soil. Polytunnels are now available with a base rail and a clip infill to secure and tension the polythene, thus avoiding the need for trenching. They are secured by being fixed to ground tubes buried in the ground or with removable ground spikes. The covers usually last for at least three seasons.

Polytunnels can suffer from condensation so it is essential to ensure adequate ventilation.

Polytunnels are available from the larger garden centres or from the Internet.

Cold frames and cloches

As an alternative to greenhouses or polytunnels, seedlings can be brought on with the use of a cold frame, and growing plants can be protected by cloches.

A cold frame is a small unheated structure used to harden off (acclimatize) young plants before planting outside, and to protect plants from frost (see Figure 11). Cold frames can also be used for growing crops such as lettuce, courgettes and other salad crops.

Cold frames are available commercially but can be constructed out of brick or, if you wish to recycle, recycled floorboards and window frames. Ventilation is important and the lid will need to be lifted as the heat of the day increases. Cold frames will not protect seedlings or tender plants from frost.

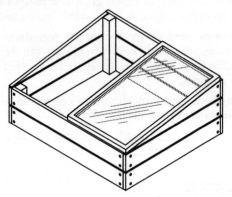

Figure 11 Cold frame

Cloches are small portable structures made of clear glass or plastic used for the protection of single plants (see Figure 12). Tunnel cloches are metal hoops covered in clear plastic film or horticultural fleece and intended to protect a row of crops.

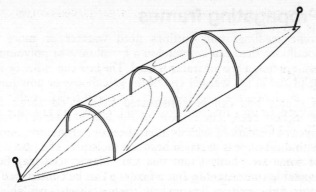

Figure 12 Plastic tunnel cloche

Top tip

'Pop' bottles (1- or 2-litre bottles) with the bottom removed make excellent cloches for individual plants.

Figure 13 Bottle cloche

Top tip

Permanent tunnel cloches can be made by bolting 3- or 4-m by 2.2-m (10- or 13-ft by 7-ft) lengths of MDPE polyethylene water pipe (available from builder's merchants) to laths and then covering with either polythene, horticultural fleece or netting. These can then be used to cover 1.2-m (4-ft) wide raised beds.

Propagating frames

Some seedlings and cuttings need warmer or more moist conditions than can be found in a greenhouse or polytunnel. To achieve this, a box or frame is used. The box can either be heated or placed at the warmer end of the greenhouse or polytunnel.

A simple box can be constructed from wood about 15 cm (6 inches) deep. The bottom of the box is then covered by a layer of insulation, such as a flat sheet of polystyrene, and filled with sand or peat to retain heat and moisture. The pots or trays of seeds are plunged into this box. Plastic seed tray lids are available commercially, but a box top can be constructed using clear, twin wall, polypropylene roofing sheets (available from most DIY stores) for the sides and top. Alternatively, loops of stiff wire made from old coat hangers can be fixed to the box and then covered in clear polythene.

An unheated box will still provide a higher temperature than the greenhouse itself, but you will need to check the temperature in hot weather to avoid overheating.

Fruit cages

Rather than lose your fruit to the birds, protection can be afforded either by draping anti-bird netting over the individual plants or by erecting a fruit cage to house all your fruit bushes and plants. Commercial fruit cages are available, but with some ingenuity they can be constructed by making a frame from fairly inexpensive materials, such as treated roofing laths, and then covering this with netting.

Site and plot security

Allotment sites are, by their very nature, difficult to secure adequately. Often sited on the outskirts of towns and villages, and not overlooked sufficiently by housing, they can become the target of thieves and vandals.

To help protect the site, it is important to ensure that any fencing or hedging surrounding it is kept in good repair and condition. If the maintenance of the perimeter of the site is the responsibility of the landlord, ensure he or she is made aware of any problems or damage so that it can be repaired as a matter of urgency.

If the site has lockable gates, make sure they are always locked when leaving the site, as an unlocked gate does not provide an adequate deterrent.

Keep the site and your plot tidy – a site that appears well used is less likely to be attacked than one that is scruffy and looks as if people rarely set foot on it.

Top security tips

- Take your tools home with you or lock them securely in a shed, preferably out of sight, to remove temptation from an opportunistic thief.
- Do not leave things on your plot that are valuable or that you cannot afford to lose.
- Mark your tools with some form of identification, such as your postcode, to make them less attractive to thieves but easier to identify and recover.
- Fit a battery-operated burglar alarm to your shed, but ensure it does not become a nuisance if it is activated. Always make arrangements for it to be turned off as soon as possible.
- If your site is overlooked by houses, try to encourage neighbouring householders to telephone and report any incidents to a named plotholder. To keep them interested in continuing to help and to thank the householder, you could give them a box of produce.
- All incidents should be reported to the police to enable them to take action if the incidents increase.

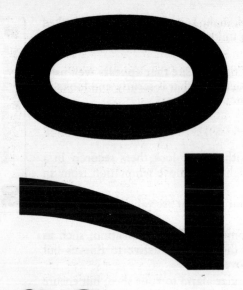

07

children and allotments

In this chapter you will learn:
• how to interest children in
  growing on your allotment.

Children are the future of gardening, and this is particularly so with allotment gardening. It has been widely publicized that the diets of many children can be low in fruit and vegetables, and it is important that they are encouraged to eat healthier foods.

Providing children with their own patch of soil not only keeps them occupied, but teaches them where food comes from and helps them to appreciate the difference in taste between fresh produce and that which has travelled thousands of miles around the world.

Growing food also presents opportunities for children to find out about pollination, germination and how crops mature, as well as the parts that wildlife and nature play in the whole gardening process. In addition, digging and raking the soil provides children with healthy exercise.

Unfortunately, vegetables do not seem to be as attractive and interesting to children as convenience meals, and many parents feel they have to disguise them to ensure they are eaten as part of a balanced diet. By encouraging children to garden and grow food themselves, they are more inclined to try what they have grown, and thereby become more appreciative of what they are eating.

Getting children involved

As the interest and attention span of children tend to be limited, it is better to provide them with small plots that can be prepared and planted in a short space of time. It is possibly better to make some small raised beds, approximately 1 sq m (3 sq ft), as this will enable the children to work easily from the path. A raised bed system avoids treading on the plot too much, which makes it easier for children to dig and prepare for sowing. With the annual addition of compost to the bed, it should be possible to eventually have a plot that will not need major digging on a regular basis.

Start with simple crops that are quick growing, as children are often impatient and want to see results immediately. With smaller children it is better to mix in a few flowers such as nasturtiums and sunflowers. Potatoes and pumpkins are always popular vegetables for children to grow, but they can take up space. Radishes are quick and easy to grow, but are often too peppery for children and it is better for them to grow something they like or are prepared to eat.

Runner beans and French beans can be linked to *Jack and the Beanstalk*, a story with which most small children are familiar. These are very simple to grow, but impressive results can be achieved if using a cane wigwam.

Onion sets, once planted, will be seen growing right the way through to maturity and harvest. Spring onions grown from seed are not quite so obvious initially, but can be harvested as an earlier crop leaving space for a later additional crop.

Potatoes can be planted singly in a 30-cm (12-inch) or larger container to provide a small supply of baby potatoes.

Some parents may feel they do not have sufficient time to involve their children with helping on a plot. However, with some advance planning it can be manageable, although you will need to be flexible as children might not always want to go with you.

Choose a time when your children will be more interested such as summer evenings when their homework is done or Saturday mornings and Sunday afternoons. Ensure you have an activity available for when they are not occupied on their own plot, such as weeding, competitions to find and identify the most weeds, and spotting and identifying wildlife, especially insects.

If there are several families with children on your site, see if there is a spare piece of ground available to act as a play area, but speak to your landlord or allotment association before proceeding.

If you have teenagers, encourage them to bring their friends along to help out, and reward them with your surplus produce. This way you can help spread the healthy eating message.

Older children and young adults, under 18 years of age, cannot legally sign a tenancy agreement and take on an allotment in their own name. It will be necessary for a parent or guardian to act as the tenant and be responsible for complying with the terms of the agreement and for the conduct of their children.

There is no lower age limit for allowing unaccompanied children and young adults onto the plot; parents should make a decision as to how responsible the particular child is. There are a number of 12–14 year olds on allotments who are good competent gardeners and vegetable growers. See if you can find a mentor on the site who can give advice and encouragement. Surplus produce could be sold to friends and neighbours to enable the children to earn money to recoup some of their costs.

Top tip
Don't worry about children getting dirty – it soon washes off!

08

livestock and wildlife on allotments

In this chapter you will learn:
- about the requirements for keeping livestock
- how to attract beneficial wildlife to your plot
- about whether or not to spray.

Livestock

While owning livestock might seem idyllic and rewarding, particularly where children are involved, you will need to seriously consider whether you have sufficient commitment, time, expertise and resources to keep them on your allotment before proceeding.

Keeping livestock can be rewarding in terms of interacting with nature in addition to producing eggs, milk or honey. However, there are many disadvantages as you will need to check on your livestock at least once a day (including Christmas and bank holidays) to ensure that they have sufficient water and food available. You will also need to find someone willing and reliable to look after your livestock when you want to go away on holiday.

The 1950 Allotment Act permits an allotment tenant to keep hens and rabbits as a right, as long as they are for the tenant's own use and are not kept or used for trade or business purposes. However, they must not be kept in such a condition as to be a health hazard or to create a nuisance or to affect their well-being.

The keeping of other livestock, such as goats, pigs and bees, are considered a reasonable use of an allotment plot, but can only be kept with the consent of the landowner, who may make such rules and conditions as is thought necessary. If you are considering such livestock, contact your landlord and put any request for approval in writing.

It must be remembered that all forms of livestock are now subject to welfare codes for housing and feeding, etc. Consequently, it is advisable to obtain relevant information and details of any regulations issued by the Department for Environment, Food and Rural Affairs (DEFRA) or the Royal Society for the Prevention of Cruelty to Animals (RSPCA) before embarking on livestock keeping.

Animals should not be kept unless they are provided with an appropriate environment and adequate general care. You will need to consider that you might need a vet if your livestock becomes ill and this, together with other ongoing expenses, could be costly.

Hens

Hens are the most popular livestock kept on allotments as they provide a supply of fresh free-range eggs. It must be made clear that 'hens' refers to the female of the species and does not include the keeping of cockerels. The latter are often covered by local bylaws because they tend to be noisy when crowing at sunrise, which will soon infuriate neighbouring householders and will create a noise nuisance that is an offence and actionable by the council.

Hens will eat waste vegetables and kitchen scraps and the resultant manure will benefit the compost heap and vegetable plot.

It must be remembered that hens are living creatures that have their own needs, and so need looking after. They cannot just be turned out onto the plot to do their own thing. A daily inspection is necessary to ensure they remain healthy and have sufficient food and drink available and are not suffering from predators, disease and/or parasites. Are you prepared for this?

There are a number of legal welfare standards for commercial flocks, and these should also be applied to domestic poultry-keeping to ensure the birds are kept healthy and happy.

Before you buy any hens or equipment, make sure you've done your research. To find out what is involved, read books, look online and chat with other plotholders who have chickens.

Choosing your hens

There are many different breeds of hens available, from the pure or rare breeds to crosses that have been bred to produce specific characteristics such as meat quality or increased egg production. Breeds are also characterized by size, ranging from Bantams, which are small birds, to 'large fowl', which produce a greater amount of eggs, to heavy breeds for meat production. The smaller the bird, the smaller their eggs, but larger birds will need more space and food. Check out Internet sites and select a breed to most suit your needs and the available space.

Ex-battery hens are also available and tend to be less expensive. They are perfectly capable of continuing in egg production for two or three years, but will need a rest period before coming back into production. You will also need to remember that hens eventually stop laying eggs, at which time you have to consider whether to dispose of them or to keep them purely as pets.

Premises with more than 50 birds must now be registered with the GB Poultry Register at DEFRA but, as hens on an allotment are intended for the use of the plotholder only, it is unlikely that you will be contemplating keeping such a large number.

Remember, hens require fresh air, access to clean water and food at all times, and shelter from the cold, rain, wind, sun and excessive heat. They will also require sufficient space to grow, exercise, sleep and lay eggs. The birds also need to be kept disease-free and safe from predators.

Check to ensure your plot is suitable for keeping hens. Is it near a main road? Does it have a suitable fence? Is it big enough? Is there a problem with foxes on the site?

Recommended stocking densities

Housing

Hens are usually housed at night to protect them from predators and allowed to roam free to forage during the day.

The number of birds that can be housed will be determined by the shed size, based on perch space per bird. Hens need 15–18 cm (6–7 inches) perch space per bird; perches should be 3–5 cm (1–2 inches) wide with round edges. Perches should be sited at 30 cm (12 inches) horizontal spacing with 20 cm (8 inches) between the perch and the wall and at least 60 cm (24 inches) off the ground.

The floor area should be covered with straw or wood shavings, etc., which can then be cleaned out on a regular basis and added to the compost heap.

Nest boxes, at least one per seven birds, should be fixed in such a way as to allow easy access for egg collection and cleaning. They should be lined with clean and dry materials, such as straw or wood shavings, and cleaned out on a regular basis. Nest boxes should be large enough to enable the hen to stand comfortably and turn around easily.

Good ventilation is necessary to bring in fresh air and to remove carbon dioxide, heat and ammonia. For small hen houses, windows or vents on one side of the house are normally sufficient.

Hens generate their own body heat and it is important that the house does not get excessively hot, particularly in summer. As a rough guide, if the temperature is not comfortable for you then the hens are likely to be suffering as well.

A 6-ft by 4-ft (2-sq m) shed will house a maximum of 20–25 hens.

Alternatively, moveable poultry arks can be used, usually with approximately six birds per ark. Arks are available commercially or you can make your own. There are a number of websites selling books and plans.

Outdoor space

The number of birds you can keep on your plot will depend on the housing available, as mentioned above, but hens also need outside space.

To avoid a build-up of disease, and damage to the soil, it is advisable to have at least two paddocks or pens available for alternate use, to allow the ground to have a period of rest to allow the soil and grass to recover. As hens like to have shade and shelter during the day, fruit trees could be planted in each pen to enable the hens to feed on pests as well as to shelter from the sun and rain.

Hens like to dust-bathe to help them to remove parasites in the feathers and on the skin, so a sunny area specifically allocated for this purpose should be provided or made available. A large shallow box filled with fine sand or sifted earth would be suitable, but make sure it is covered to prevent the sand or earth getting wet.

Current commercial free-range stocking density requirements approved by the European Union (EU) are 1,010 birds per acre which equates to 2.5 birds per square metre (10 sq ft). The RSPCA recommends 404 birds per acre which equates to 1 bird per square metre (10 sq ft). This indicates that each 2-sq m (6-ft by 4-ft) shed will require a paddock or preferably two paddocks of between 10 and 25 sq m (100 and 250 sq ft).

Each paddock will need to be fenced, not only to keep the hens in but also to keep predators out. A fine mesh or chicken wire fence should be erected with the wire buried outward and at an angle, at least 60 cm (24 inches) deep, to stop predators from digging under the fence.

Hens will need to be shut in at night and let out in the morning.

Food and water

It is essential that hens have access to clean water at all times. Suitable water containers and drinkers are available commercially, which ensure that the water is kept clean and also prevent the hens from drowning, especially when young.

Hens spend much of the day scratching for seeds, roots, vegetation and insects in the ground, but will require additional feed, such as grain, to make sure they have a balanced diet. In particular, laying hens require a calcium supplement for the production of egg shell in addition to the protein, carbohydrates and minerals that all birds require. Hens will also need access to insoluble grit to help with their digestion process. It is therefore advisable to supplement their diet with commercial hen food (mash), which is also available as a 'layers' mash with all the nutritional requirements included for egg production.

Hens will also eat green leafy vegetation, such as the outer leaves of cabbages, which needs to be secured and can be tied to the fence. Hens will eat kitchen scraps, but meat products should be avoided as these can attract vermin.

All food should be kept in a dry container that is rodent-proof to avoid contamination.

Bee-keeping

Bees are an essential part of gardening as they help to pollinate fruit and seed crops such as beans. They are, therefore, extremely beneficial to allotment sites. Better yields and quality produce will result from having hives sited nearby.

In practice, bees need to be protected from the public rather than the other way around, so location is important.

- Bee-keeping on allotments should only be carried out by experienced keepers, who should also be members of the British Beekeepers' Association. Membership of this organization includes third-party insurance cover.
- Inexperienced beekeepers should only be allowed to keep hives if they have the benefit of guidance and supervision from an experienced keeper.
- Hives are best sited away from other plotholders and in the centre of the plot.
- The bees should be forced to fly above 1.8 m (6 ft) before leaving the plot by the use of hedges, fencing or screens to encourage them to forage further for food, and they should avoid flight paths that will impinge on other plotholders.
- Always ensure that someone else is on site in case of an emergency when handling bees.
- The number of colonies in any area should be limited.
- Only obtain bees from a reputable source.

Ensure potential neighbouring plotholders are not allergic to bee stings before deciding on a final location for the hives.

For further information, contact the British Beekeepers' Association (see the 'Taking it further' section for details).

Other livestock

Livestock, such as pigs and goats, have in the past been kept on allotments, but recent outbreaks of Foot and Mouth disease have resulted in strict laws and regulations being applied, even if you only keep one animal. DEFRA is the first port of call to check on the current regulations (see the 'Taking it further' section for details).

At the time of writing, before moving stock onto your plot you will need a County Parish Holding number to identify your premises. You will then need to obtain a stock movement licence from whoever is selling the animals. You will even need a 'walking' licence if you wish to take your goat for a walk.

Once the stock is on your holding, you need to register them with DEFRA. It is also necessary to keep accurate official records of all such livestock kept on the holding as this will make it easier to trace the source and movement of stock in the event of highly contagious viruses.

Your records will include the following:

- the date of the movement
- the identification mark and herd number
- number of animals on the holding
- the holding from which the stock was moved
- the holding to which stock is moved.

In the event of a local Foot and Mouth outbreak, you may find that access to the site by other plotholders will be prohibited and this needs to be taken into consideration.

Pig- or goat-keeping is a specialist activity that should not be undertaken lightly. The subject will need to be researched thoroughly and discussed with your landlord before considering such a venture.

Wildlife

Whether you intend to be an organic gardener or to use chemicals, it is important to garden in a way that respects and protects nature both in terms of the living organisms and the environment in general.

Many birds, animals and insects live off the very pests that the gardener wants destroyed such as aphid, slugs and caterpillars. You can encourage such beneficial creatures to assist you with pest control by creating habitats and an environment that will attract them to your plot and site.

Allotment sites present many opportunities for attracting the 'right kind' of wildlife that is struggling to survive on modern farmland and in cities and concreted-over gardens. Wildlife habitats can be provided by individual plotholders, but the whole allotment site will supply more opportunities for larger projects, and perhaps enable a shallow pond to be built on wasteland or surplus plots to attract frogs and toads.

Ideal wildlife habitats include:

- hedges and trees
- ponds
- nest boxes
- bat boxes
- beetle banks/bug hotels
- piles of logs or stones – these make suitable habitats for hedgehogs, frogs and toads.

Derelict areas or the site margins can be used as wildlife areas by growing wild flowers, brambles and nettles. However, it must be stressed that such areas cannot just be left to 'go wild'; they need to be managed or they will get away, become overgrown, affect or encroach on other plots, and can look untidy.

Birds

With the exception of wood pigeons, which tend to eat young brassicas, most birds, particularly the insect eaters, are beneficial to the vegetable and fruit plot.

- Blackbirds and starlings will eat fruit, which will need to be protected with netting, but they also eat snails, slugs and other insects.

- Blue tits feed on aphid, caterpillars and other insects.
- Thrushes feed on snails, insects and their larvae.
- Robins feed on insects and larvae.
- House sparrows feed on grain, weed seeds, insects and their larvae.

Insects

Beneficial insects include the following:

- Bees, which are the number one pollinator.
- Centipedes feed on ground-dwelling insects and eat slugs and their eggs.
- Earwigs, which although are often regarded as pests, eat caterpillars and vine weevil eggs.
- Ground beetles, including the devil's coach-horse, prey on slugs.
- Hoverfly larvae, lacewing, and ladybirds and their larvae prey on aphid.
- Spiders eat flies and other insects.
- Tachnid flies, which look like versions of the housefly, feed on butterfly and moth caterpillars, sawflies and aphid.
- Even the much maligned wasp feeds on insect larvae and caterpillars.

Organic or inorganic?

Unless your site has collectively made a decision to garden on organic principles, the decision whether or not to use chemicals is a matter for the individual. If other plotholders are spraying all the time, it can be difficult being completely organic as the pests tend to make a 'bee line' for the untreated plot.

A large majority of allotment gardeners do not use herbicides (weedkillers), pesticides or fungicides at all, but those who do tend to use them to treat a problem rather than use them as a preventative measure.

Many plotholders try organic methods first, such as washing aphid off with soapy water, but if the problem persists to the extent that the crops are likely to be harmed then they are more inclined to resort to chemical remedies.

If you are considering using chemicals, it is advisable to follow the 'Helpful Hints on Using Garden Pesticides' produced by the

Pesticides Safety Directorate (see the 'Taking it further' section for further details).

As most chemical ingredients are non-specific, they will kill friend and foe alike. This means that any new infestation will be free to destroy your crops as there will be no predators available, and further treatment will become necessary.

09

allotment and gardening associations

In this chapter you will learn:
- about the benefits of allotment associations
- how to form and run an association
- what self-management means.

The benefits of forming an allotment association

Allotment gardening can be a sole activity carried out by an individual plotholder without the need to involve or make contact with anyone else. While this can allow plotholders to enjoy peace, quiet and solitude, they will miss out on sharing their interest with, and learning from, others. Gardening, and in particular food growing, should be enjoyed in the company of others. You can also share surplus produce, plants and knowledge. Moreover, gardening is an activity in which all the family can participate.

Allotment gardening helps to create a community spirit as it takes no account of class, creed or race. Everyone is interested in the same goal, which is to provide sufficient fresh wholesome food for themselves and their family, and often for friends and neighbours as well. Membership of an allotment association will help to tie all of this together and enables members to work in cooperation with each other and to the same end.

An allotment association is run by its members and therefore speaks (hopefully) with one voice, making it easier to resolve problems, speak to the landlord, arrange for the purchase of horticultural supplies in bulk (and at discounted prices), and arrange communal activities such as barbeques, open days, plant and produce swaps, etc. For a well-run and active association, the opportunities are endless.

Many allotment associations take on self-management, where they accept some of the responsibility of running the site. This can have many benefits such as ensuring that vacant plots are filled quickly and repairs and maintenance are carried out as soon as is required.

Self-management schemes need the support of all plotholders to ensure the smooth running of the site. The association will, however, require third-party and/or public liability insurance to insure it against claims for accidental damage or injury.

The essentials of forming an association

Enthusiasm and support from the plotholders is very important, for without it an association is likely to struggle. Such enthusiasm will stem from those inspired by the array of possibilities that an association can bring to a site, and who are able to pass that enthusiasm on to others.

If there is no existing association on your site, start by inviting all plotholders to a meeting to allow everyone to discuss the idea and to resolve any questions or problems that might arise. Many groups arrange such meetings in a pub or church hall, initially on an informal basis.

Once it is agreed that an association should be formed, either a further formal meeting could be arranged to elect a committee and officers, or if those in attendance agree, the election of the initial committee could be made at that initial meeting.

The committee

While the talk of a committee structure might seem too formal and daunting, in reality it need only be as complex as circumstances require, and it can be built upon over a period of time.

The minimum requirements should be:

- a secretary to handle correspondence, arrange and record meetings and decisions made
- a chairman to conduct meetings to ensure every member is given a voice, and to ensure the affairs of the association are being conducted properly
- a treasurer responsible for association funds.

It is also advisable to have a further four to six committee members to ensure a good balanced representation.

The first committee can be a provisional group working to get the association up and running, with the option of retiring once this has been put into effect.

Top tip

While qualifications and committee experience are an advantage, an ability and willingness to carry out the role can be more important. Experience can be learnt, and advice can always be found on the Internet or from representative organizations.

The first formal meeting

At the first formal meeting it will be necessary to decide on a constitution (basic rules as to how the association will operate and what it intends to do as an organization). Model rules are available from the National Society of Allotment and Leisure Gardeners Ltd at **www.nsalg.org.uk**.

Discussion will also be needed on how the association will be funded and what activities or projects it wishes to implement or support. Local grant funding may be available for some projects or start-up costs, and the sale of seeds and horticultural supplies to members will also provide an opportunity for a small profit towards association funds. The local volunteer centre may be able to provide advice on available local funding. Annual members' subscriptions will also help to raise funds.

Further committee meetings should be arranged as and when required, where the business of the association can be discussed and decided upon.

It will be necessary to hold meetings of the members at least once a year to enable the committee to report on what has been done and achieved during the past 12 months, what it is looking to achieve in the following year, and how the finances are holding up.

Annual or general meetings are times for all the members to get together to discuss the future working of the association, which will benefit the members as a whole group. Often, associations will use such meetings as an opportunity to gather socially (after the formal business part of the meeting) and enjoy each other's company.

The elected committee should meet on a regular basis, but especially when important matters arise and need consideration. A minor problem can soon become major if left for too long before being resolved.

While formal meetings are conducted in a business-like fashion so that every member has an opportunity to express their views, membership of an association should be fun and enjoyable so that every member derives some benefit from their membership.

Joint activities

Before organizing any event, ensure you have the permission of the landlord and that there is sufficient public liability insurance cover in place. Check with your landlord to see if such cover already exists, but if not your association will need to arrange its own cover. Avoid events or activities that might present a danger to members or to the public, and ensure there are no dangerous structures or items lying around that might cause injury.

Events will benefit from detailed planning to make sure they are successful. It is useful if volunteers can be found to accept responsibility for various aspects of the event such as ticket sales, making posters, health and safety issues, refreshments and entertainment, etc. Not everyone will possess the necessary skills for such jobs, but most people can make cups of tea and coffee, prepare sandwiches, litter-pick, and carry out the many simple yet important jobs that help 'make' an event, so everyone should be encouraged to participate. The more people that get involved, the easier the event will be to organize and the more successful it will be, with everyone, including the 'volunteers', having an enjoyable time.

Self-management

Originally, all individual allotment plot tenants rented their plots directly from their local authority. The local authority maintained waiting lists, let plots, terminated tenancies and carried out repairs and improvements to sites. Such arrangements are usually referred to as 'Directly Administered Sites', with tenancies being granted by the landlord to the tenant on an annual basis.

Self-management schemes (sometimes referred to as 'devolved management') are regarded by many as beneficial to allotment associations, plotholders and local authorities.

The basic form of self-administration is when an organized association (one with a properly constitutional set of rules, and an elected committee) collects rent from each plotholder and makes an agreed payment to the local authority. Normally these associations maintain waiting lists, let plots and, in most cases, monitor the cultivation of plots and terminate tenancies if and when necessary. Such management schemes save local authorities considerable administration time and costs, which is reflected in a lower overall rent charge to the association or in a payment or percentage allowance of the total site rent going directly to the association.

Generally, the association leases the site from the local authority on a longer term basis, with reasonable conditions and safeguards for each party. More progressive systems are tailored to give more responsibility to associations, either on an individual site basis or on a district or similar collective group of associations. The associations take on various maintenance works such as grass and hedge cutting, minor repairs, and painting, etc. Some schemes operate on a rent credit system whereby the local authority allows the allotment association to retain all or part of the yearly rent; others charge a reduced or peppercorn rent to allow the allotment association to charge individual members an amount sufficient to cover the cost of managing the site.

There are many extensions to self-help schemes, all designed to give greater responsibility to allotment associations and to reduce the involvement and expenses of local authorities, thereby allowing a larger budget to be spent on the sites and provision.

There are many local authorities that provide the materials required for improvements and maintenance to sites, allowing the members to provide the labour for carrying out the work. Others agree a total self-management system whereby all the sites within a district are leased on a long-term basis to a single organization, which then determines the rent level to be paid by individuals and/or sites. The collective rent is then used by the allotment organization to carry out development and maintenance of the sites under their control. The local authority may also offer an agreed additional sum of money or a substantial amount of materials to assist with the management of the sites.

The more progressive schemes of self-management usually evolve from a lesser responsibility scheme after a period of 'ability to manage' has been shown by an association.

It is clear that the plotholders on a site tend to be instantly aware of vacancies occurring, overgrown plots, site repair and maintenance needs and, if it is within their responsibility, they will respond almost instantly to deal with most situations or problems. A local authority, by its very nature and with its chain of procedure in dealing with problems and issues, is bound to involve cost and to take considerably longer to respond and act.

Essentials to be aware of

No self-management scheme can work successfully if an 'us and them' attitude exists on the site. Any progress or agreement needs complete trust and confidence between all parties involved, whether local authority, association committee or plotholder.

A survey of the site or sites should be carried out to determine the condition of fences/boundaries, gates, roadways and paths, etc., and to assess the possible near-future expenditure required. The association can reach agreement with the landlord regarding the provision of materials and/or capital to enable repairs and maintenance to be undertaken before any lease is signed. It does not make sense for an association to take on responsibility for a site that already has outstanding maintenance problems.

There is a need for a continuity of officers of the association with sufficient competence and commitment to carry out administration, and the ability to organize and motivate a team of similarly dedicated members. It is no good depending on one or two people to do everything, nor is it practical to frequently change the officers or committee.

It is also essential that all officers are elected by and are answerable to the members.

Remember, safety is a must at all times. Proper equipment and materials, and the provision of safety clothing where required, is paramount. Adequate insurance cover must also be in place, including public and products liability cover and possibly personal injury cover for helpers, in addition to cover for machinery and equipment. If the association pays for someone to carry out a job, it may also require employer's liability insurance cover.

There are some tasks that site members should not undertake unless it is their normal trade or profession, for example, the felling of diseased trees or the erection of sectional concrete buildings and electrical installations.

When negotiating agreements, conditions and responsibilities, be mindful of various safeguards. A total site charge is fine if all plots are let, but it can be costly if there are a number of vacant or unusable plots, as the cost of the vacant plots may need to be shared among the other plotholders and members on site. This not only means higher rents and potentially lower income to the association, but often results in the need for higher maintenance with less help available. Ask the landlord to make an allowance for any unused plots until such a time when they can be let.

Longer term leases with medium-term break clauses (a mid-term review) are essential safety nets in case the association no longer feels capable of carrying out the management of the site and wishes to transfer management back to the landlord or to renegotiate the terms of the lease.

Short-term leases do not allow an association to plan management and improvements for the long term.

A reduction in rent for pensioners and others on reduced income, or for those disadvantaged or with disabilities, is often given by local authorities and will need to be considered by the managing association.

Many associations and members are content to leave everything to their local authority; others are not. Similarly, many local authorities are keen to transfer their responsibility, but others are not. The question to ask is: What do your members feel is the best route for them?

Self-management is all about teamwork and mutual benefit. Some successful self-help schemes have produced a wonderful social attitude among their members and recreated a spirit of belonging to and working with the community.

10

the allotment gardening year

In this chapter you will learn:
- what to do when throughout the year.

The following seed sowing and planting out times refer to a temperate climate. However, the further north you live in the UK could make as much as four weeks' difference. Read the seed packet instructions for full details, and keep an eye on what others are doing locally and on your own weather conditions.

January

Things to do: If you do not have an allotment association on your site, or your association does not run a discounted seed scheme, then obtain some mail order seed catalogues and decide what seeds you want to order.

Crop maintenance: Keep brassicas clean and remove dead leaves to avoid harbouring pests.

Sow: Summer cabbages and cauliflowers, and tomatoes under heat (in a propagator, heated greenhouse or kitchen or on a warm windowsill), lettuce under glass (in a greenhouse or polytunnel).

Harvest: Brussels sprouts, celery, Jerusalem artichokes, kale, leeks, winter cabbages. Buy and 'chit' seed potatoes.

February

Things to do: Apply fertilizer to overwintered crops and to ground ready to be sown with early crops. Dig the ground if it is dry.

Crop maintenance: Cut down autumn fruiting raspberry canes and tie new canes to the wires as they grow.

Sow: Broad beans, summer cabbages, cauliflowers under glass, cucumbers and lettuce under glass, onion seed, parsnips, peas, and tomatoes under heat.

Plant out: Jerusalem artichokes, onion sets.

Harvest: Broccoli, Brussels sprouts, winter cabbages, celery, kale, leeks.

March

Things to do: Dig over the soil if you have not done so earlier, and prepare for sowing.

Crop maintenance: Thin and weed onions; hoe weeds generally. Transplant seedlings sown earlier, but keep under cover until all risk of frost has passed.

Sow: Broad beans, broccoli, Brussels sprouts, summer cabbages, carrots, and celery under cover, cucumbers under glass, leeks, peas, radishes, tomatoes under cover in a greenhouse, turnips and swedes.

Plant out: Asparagus crowns, globe artichoke offsets, onion sets, shallots and garlic, and early potatoes.

Harvest: Broccoli, kale, leeks.

April

Things to do: Cover brassicas with fine netting to keep off cabbage white butterflies.

Crop maintenance: Hoe weeds, weed onions by hand to avoid disturbance to the roots.

Sow: Beetroot, broad beans, broccoli, Brussels sprouts, summer and winter cabbages, carrots, celery under cover, cucumbers under glass, kale, French beans under cover, marrows/courgettes/squashes under cover in a greenhouse or polytunnel, peas, radishes, tomatoes under cover, turnips and swedes, winter cabbages.

Plant out: Globe artichoke offsets, asparagus crowns, cucumbers under glass, onion sets, shallots and garlic, maincrop potatoes and any hardy vegetables started indoors once the risk of frost has gone.

Harvest: Broccoli, spring cabbages.

May

Things to do: Stake peas and runner beans. Watch for blackfly attacking broad beans.

Crop maintenance: Hoe weeds, weed onions by hand. Place straw under strawberries to keep soil off the fruit. Draw soil over the emerging shoots of potatoes (earth up), especially in frosty weather.

Sow: Beetroot, broad beans, Brussels sprouts, carrots, and cucumbers under glass, French beans, kale, marrows/courgettes/squashes, peas, runner beans, sweetcorn, turnips and swedes, winter cabbages.

Plant out: Globe artichoke offsets, broccoli, cucumbers, potatoes, tomatoes.

Harvest: Asparagus, broad beans, spring cabbages, radishes, winter sown peas, lettuce and salad leaves and spring onions.

June

Things to do: Stake runner beans. Tie in tomatoes.

Crop maintenance: Hoe weeds, weed onions by hand.

Sow: French beans, kale, radishes, runner beans, turnips and swedes.

Plant out: Broccoli, Brussels sprouts, celery, cucumbers, leeks, sweetcorn, and tomatoes.

Harvest: Asparagus, broad beans, early potatoes, radishes, winter sown peas, lettuce.

July

Things to do: Cut down raspberry canes that have fruited, and tie in the new cane growth.

Crop maintenance: Hoe weeds, earth up maincrop potatoes.

Sow: Spring cabbages, radishes.

Plant out: Brussels sprouts, kale, leeks.

Harvest: Broad beans, cauliflowers, French beans, globe artichokes, runner beans, marrows and courgettes, peas, potatoes, radishes, summer cabbages, strawberries, raspberries, currants and rhubarb.

August

Things to do: If your allotment association runs a discounted seed scheme, ask your secretary if the catalogues and order forms are available. Enjoy planning what you could grow next year. Prepare new strawberry beds and transplant new runners produced by the older plants. Transplant winter and spring cauliflowers.

Crop maintenance: Earth up non self-blanching celery. Hoe weeds. Keep an eye open for potato and tomato blight. Weed carrots. Dry onions prior to storage.

Sow: Cabbages, spinach, winter lettuces, onions.

Harvest: Globe artichokes, beetroot, cucumbers, broad beans, French beans, runner beans, peas, summer cabbages, cauliflowers, onions, sweetcorn, tomatoes.

September

Things to do: Check which seeds you already have a sufficient quantity of, and select those that you need to buy. Ensure you get your order back to the allotment secretary by the end of the month, if possible, to enable the association to take advantage of any discounts available. If this is your first season purchasing seeds, make certain that you only order or purchase what you need as it is very easy to get carried away and buy too much.

Cut off this year's fruiting blackberry canes and tie in new cane growth. Order new fruit bushes.

Crop maintenance: Keep hoeing weeds.

Sow: Cauliflower, Swiss chard, perpetual spinach.

Plant out: Spring cabbages, chicory, perpetual spinach.

Harvest: Beetroot, broad beans, globe artichokes, Jerusalem artichokes, cucumbers, French beans, runner beans, marrows and courgettes, onions, parsnips, peas, potatoes, radishes, summer cabbages, sweetcorn, turnips and swedes.

October

Things to do: Dig over heavy soils. Manure the potato plot ready for spring planting.

Crop maintenance: Protect late cauliflowers from frost damage by leaves broken from the plants.

Sow: Broad bean overwintering varieties, peas under cover.

Plant out: Spring cabbages, Japanese onion sets.

Harvest: Beetroot, Brussels sprouts, carrots, cucumbers, Jerusalem artichokes, onions, parsnips, peas, potatoes, turnips and swedes, and store as required.

Leave crops such as cabbages, celeriac, Jerusalem artichokes, kale and parsnips in the ground and harvest as required.

November

Things to do: Autumn digging before winter sets in. Dig manure into the legumes bed.

Crop maintenance: Protect globe artichoke crowns with straw. Cut fern-like growth from asparagus.

Sow: Broad beans overwintering varieties, peas under cover.

Plant out: Garlic cloves, new rhubarb crowns.

Harvest: Remaining beetroot for winter storage, Brussels sprouts, carrots, celery, Jerusalem artichokes, leeks, winter cabbages, cauliflowers.

December

Things to do: Look at your record of crops and make notes on any necessary changes that need to be made.

Crop maintenance: There is not much to do this month apart from harvesting winter produce and enjoying a well-earned rest ready for the New Year.

Plant out: Onion sets.

Harvest: Jerusalem artichokes, Brussels sprouts, cauliflowers, celery, kale, leeks, winter cabbages.

Top tips for a successful year

- Protect new plants with cloches (2-litre fizzy drink bottles with the bottoms cut off make excellent cloches for single plants).
- Raise plants in pots to produce strong plants before transplanting them into the growing site.
- Keep a written note of what you have planted and where, as labels don't always stay put in windy weather! This can also help you with planning for the following year.
- Hoeing in dry weather ensures the weeds will die.
- Start a compost bin immediately and recycle as much organic matter as possible.
- Use a water butt to collect rainwater from the shed or greenhouse roof, but do not use this water for watering seeds as algae growth can inhibit germination.
- Grow annual and perennial flowers as these attract pest-eating insects which are important if you are gardening organically. They also look good in a vase!

recipes

In this chapter you will learn:
- some simple but tasty recipes using your own produce.

This chapter provides a number of simple recipes to enable you to produce some tasty meals from your home-grown produce. The recipes are arranged in alphabetical order.

Recipes, like gardening, are not intended to be followed in fine detail and some ingredients can be substituted for others, depending on what is being harvested at a particular point in time. Some recipes also deal with the inevitable surplus of produce that every vegetable and fruit grower has at some time during the growing year.

Apple tart

Serves 4

750 g (1½ lb) cooking apples peeled, cored and chopped
2 tbsp caster sugar
30 g (1 oz) butter
½ tsp ground cinnamon
½ tsp ground nutmeg
1 tsp lemon juice
1 tsp brandy
250 g (9 oz) shortcrust pastry

For the topping:

3–4 apples (cooking or eating) peeled, cored and sliced thinly
Caster sugar for sprinkling
3 tbsp apricot jam, sieved

Place the chopped cooking apples in a heavy-based saucepan with a little water to prevent burning, and cook over a medium heat, stirring frequently, until the apples are soft. Keep adding small amounts of water if necessary. Some cooking apples break down into a purée, but if not, process in a blender.

Return to the saucepan and add the sugar, butter, spices, lemon juice and brandy and simmer over a low heat until the mixture forms a thick paste.

Roll out the pastry to 5 mm (¼ inch) thick and large enough to line a 23-cm (9-inch) flan tin or pie dish. Place the pastry in the tin, prick it with a fork, and line with non-stick baking paper filled with uncooked rice. Bake at 190°C (375°F, Gas mark 5) for 15 minutes. Remove the rice and paper and cook for a further 5 minutes. Set aside to cool.

Spread the apple purée over the pastry case. Arrange the apple slices, overlapping, on top of the purée. Sprinkle with caster sugar and bake for 25 minutes (again, at 190°C, 375°F, Gas mark 5) or until the apples are tender.

To make the glaze, heat the apricot jam with 1 tbsp of water in a small saucepan over a low heat, stirring for 5 minutes or until a thick syrupy glaze forms. Brush the glaze over the hot tart and set aside to cool. Serve warm or cold.

An alternative to apricot glaze is to use a quick gel or warm clear honey.

Top tip

This recipe is particularly useful for windfall apples. The tarts can be frozen without the glaze, which can be added after the tart is reheated.

Baked aubergines, mozzarella and tomato

Serves 4

750 g (1½ lb) cherry or small tomatoes
2 large or 3 medium aubergines
Mozzarella, drained
Fresh basil leaves
Olive oil
Salt and pepper to taste

Heat the oven to 200°C (400°F, Gas mark 6). Coat the tomatoes in oil and bake for 20 minutes until soft and the skins are bursting. Meanwhile heat a grill or frying pan.

Thickly slice the aubergines crosswise, brush with oil, season, and fry or grill on both sides. Arrange the aubergines in overlapping circles in a non-stick baking tray or on a tray lined with greaseproof paper. Arrange the roasted tomatoes on top and scatter small clumps of mozzarella over them. Season to taste and bake for 5 minutes, or until the mozzarella melts. Serve with a little olive oil drizzled on top and scatter with basil leaves.

Baked potatoes

1 large potato
Topping of your choice

The traditional way to cook a baked potato is to scrub and prick the surface with a fork and place on the shelf in a preheated oven at 200°C (400°F, Gas mark 6) for 60–90 minutes until it is soft to the touch.

Baked potatoes can also be started off in a microwave oven following the manufacturer's guidelines and then finished off in the oven for 20 minutes until the skins crisp.

Once cooked, the potato can be cut in half and topped with butter and other toppings to taste. Alternatively, the cooked potato can be scooped out and mashed with a little cheese and placed back into the skin. Cover with grated cheese and return to the oven until golden brown.

Topping suggestions

Baked beans and grated cheese; Brie, stilton, or grated mature cheese; Chilli con carne; Coleslaw; Cottage cheese; Garlic mushrooms (made with mushrooms and garlic, fried, plus Dijon mustard and white wine); Scrambled egg; Tomato base and grated cheese; Tuna and sweetcorn with mayonnaise; Yoghurt (plain) with diced cucumber and onion.

Beetroot chutney

500 g (1 lb) onions, chopped
600 ml (20 fl oz) spiced white vinegar
1.5 kg (3 lb) cooked beetroot, diced in small pieces
2 tsp salt
500 g (1 lb) apples, chopped
500 g (1 lb) caster sugar

Cook the chopped onions in a saucepan with a little of the vinegar until nearly soft. Add the rest of the ingredients and thoroughly stir in the sugar. Boil steadily until the chutney is thick; pour into hot jars and seal.

Store in a cool, dark place.

Chicken casserole

Serves 4

4 chicken portions, skinned (thighs or drumsticks are ideal
for this dish)
1 large onion, peeled and chopped
250 ml (8 fl oz) red wine
1 large potato, peeled and diced
2 medium carrots, diced
1 turnip, peeled and diced (if available on the allotment)
100 g (4 oz) button mushrooms (optional)
½ tsp parsley, chopped or dried
½ tsp thyme, chopped or dried
300 ml (10 fl oz) stock
5 tbsp olive or vegetable oil
Salt and pepper to taste

Heat the oil in a frying pan and brown the chicken on all sides.
Lift the chicken out and put to one side. Put the chopped onion
in the frying pan and stir until it becomes translucent.

Return the chicken to the pan, add the red wine, and cook for
2–3 minutes, until it has reduced.

Pour the chicken, onion and red wine into a casserole dish and
add the rest of the ingredients. Cover with a lid and cook in the
oven at 180°C (350°F, Gas mark 4) for 1½ hours. Check that
the meat is cooked by piercing with a sharp knife. The juices
should run clear.

Fruit smoothie

Serves 1

350 ml (12 fl oz) orange or other fruit juice
1 banana, sliced and frozen
500 g (1 lb) soft fruit frozen (such as strawberries, raspberries,
  blackberries, blackcurrants, blueberries)

Pour the fruit juice into a food processor. Add the banana and half the fruit and process until smooth. Add the remaining fruit and process until smooth. Pour the mixture into a tall glass.

If you do not have frozen fruit, fresh fruit can be used but the mixture will need to be chilled in the freezer before serving.

Fruit, such as blackberries and raspberries, may require sieving before serving to remove the pips.

Leek and chicken pie

Serves 4

400 g (14 oz) chicken, cooked and diced
2 medium leeks, sliced
White sauce (see below)
250 g (9 oz) shortcrust or puff pastry
Egg, beaten, or milk for brushing pastry

For the white sauce:

25 g (1 oz) margarine
1 heaped tsp (15 g) flour/cornflour
300 ml (10 fl oz) milk
Salt and pepper to taste

Place a layer of cooked chicken in a buttered 20-cm (8-inch) pie dish and cover with a layer of leeks. Continue with these layers until the chicken and leeks are used up. Add the white sauce.

White sauce: Melt the margarine in a saucepan. Remove from the heat and blend in the flour or cornflour. Stir in the milk and bring to the boil. Once boiling, turn down the heat and simmer for 2 minutes while stirring. Season to taste.

Alternatives: Add cooked potatoes or substitute for the chicken if vegetarian. Use a packet white sauce or for different flavours use packet soups (make with two-thirds of the water requirement).

On a floured surface, roll out the pastry to a circle that is large enough to cover the pie dish. Damp the edges of the dish before covering with the pastry. Make a few small slits in the centre of the pastry. Brush the pastry with lightly beaten egg or milk and bake in the centre of a preheated oven at 190°C (375°F, Gas mark 5) for 25 minutes, then reduce the heat to 160°C (325°F, Gas mark 3) and bake for a further 15 minutes.

Moussaka

Serves 4

1 large onion, chopped
2 cloves garlic, crushed
500 g (1 lb) minced beef
1 tbsp tomato purée
150 ml (5 fl oz) stock
4 large aubergines cut into 4-mm (¼-inch) pieces
25 g (1 oz) butter
150 ml (5 fl oz) natural yoghurt
25 g (1 oz) plain flour/cornflour
125 g (4 oz) cheddar cheese
4 tbsp olive oil
Salt and pepper to taste

Heat 15 ml (1 tbsp) oil in a pan and gently fry the onion and garlic for 5 minutes. Add the minced beef and fry until brown. Stir in the tomato purée and stock, and season to taste. Bring this mixture to the boil and simmer for 30 minutes until the meat is tender and the liquid is almost absorbed.

Fry the aubergine slices in the remaining oil until golden, then drain on absorbent paper.

Arrange a layer of aubergines in the bottom of a large buttered ovenproof dish. Cover with a layer of the meat, another layer of aubergine, and so on until all is used up, finishing with a layer of aubergines.

Blend the yoghurt into the flour or cornflour, stir in the cheese, and season to taste.

Spread the yoghurt mixture on top of the moussaka and place in a preheated oven and bake at 180°C (350°F, Gas mark 4) for 30–40 minutes or until bubbling hot and browned.

For a vegetarian option, substitute 400 g (14 oz) of chopped tomatoes and 300 g (12 oz) of sliced courgette for the minced beef.

Onion soup

Serves 4

400 g (14 oz) onions, thinly sliced
150 ml (5 fl oz) white wine
1½ tbsp flour
1 litre (35 fl oz) stock
1 tbsp olive or vegetable oil
Salt and pepper to taste

Gently fry the onions in the oil for 5 minutes. Stir in 2 tbsp of wine and simmer for 30 minutes until the onions are soft, adding more wine as necessary.

Sprinkle the flour over the onion mix and cook for 1 minute, stirring continuously. Gradually stir in the stock and remaining wine, bring to the boil, then simmer for 15 minutes. Season to taste.

Pizza

Serves 2–4

For the topping:

400 g (14 oz) tomatoes, chopped (or 2 tomato base blocks)
50 g (2 oz) grated cheese
Olive oil to taste
Salt and pepper to taste

Optional toppings:

Mozzarella; Sliced tomatoes; Mushrooms; Onions; Sweet
pepper; Smoked sausage; Salami; Diced chicken; Tuna.

For the pizza dough:

500 g (1 lb) strong white or wholemeal flour
1 tsp fast-action dried yeast
1 tsp salt
300 ml (10 fl oz) tepid water
2 tbsp olive oil

For the topping, place the tomatoes in a pan and simmer until most of the juice has been boiled off.

To make the dough, put the flour, yeast and salt in a bowl and mix together. Make a well in the centre and add the tepid water and olive oil. Beat thoroughly with your hands until the dough leaves the sides of the bowl clean. You may need to add more water, particularly if using wholemeal flour.

Turn the dough out onto a lightly floured surface and kneed for 10 minutes until smooth and elastic. Roll out to make two 30-cm (12-inch) rounds and place on a pizza or baking tray. Spread with the tomato and add the toppings of your choice. Season with salt and pepper to taste and drizzle with olive oil. Sprinkle with the grated cheese and leave in a warm place for 20–30 minutes.

Bake in the oven at 220°C (425°F, Gas mark 7) for 20–30 minutes until golden brown and bubbling.

Potato and courgette omelette

Serves 2

225 g (½ lb) potatoes, peeled and grated
110 g (4 oz) courgettes, coarsely grated
3 eggs, beaten
2 tbsp olive oil
Salt and pepper to taste

Place the potatoes in a sieve and press out any excess moisture. Heat the oil in a large frying pan, add the potatoes and fry quickly until browned and nearly cooked. Add the courgette and cook gently for 5 minutes. Stir in the eggs and salt and pepper and cook gently until just set.

Cut into wedges and serve.

Potato bake

Serves 3

500 g (1 lb) potatoes, thinly sliced
1 large onion, thinly sliced
125 g (4 oz) natural yoghurt
125 g (4 oz) double cream
30 g (1½ oz) grated cheese
Freshly ground black pepper to taste

Layer potatoes, onions and black pepper to taste in a lightly greased ovenproof dish.

Mix the yoghurt and cream in a bowl and carefully pour the mixture over the potatoes. Sprinkle with the cheese and bake at 200°C (400°F, Gas mark 6) for 40–45 minutes until the potatoes are tender and the top is golden.

The same recipe can also be used for a cauliflower and potato bake by adding one small cauliflower broken into florets.

Ratatouille

Serves 4

2 medium onions, peeled and sliced
1 garlic clove, chopped
2 green peppers, cored, seeded and sliced
2 medium aubergines, sliced (optional)
250g (9 oz) courgettes sliced
500 g (1 lb) tomatoes, skinned and chopped
½ tsp dried basil
4 tbsp dry white wine
4 tbsp olive oil
Salt and ground pepper to taste

Cook the onion and garlic gently for approximately 5 minutes in the olive oil until the onion is transparent. Add the peppers and aubergines and fry for 3 minutes, stirring occasionally. Add the courgettes, tomatoes, seasoning, herbs and wine. Cover the pan and cook for 45 minutes or until the vegetables are tender.

Serve with pasta.

Top tip

Either fresh or frozen tomatoes can be used. To skin fresh tomatoes, place them in a bowl, cover with boiling water, then remove them and place them in cold water. The skins will now be easy to remove. With frozen tomatoes, put them in very hot water for the skins to lift.

Top tip

Try adding a can of tuna (drained) just before serving. Add other leftover vegetables as well.

Sausages with oven-roasted vegetables

Serves 4

8 of your favourite sausages
8 shallots or small onions, halved
4 garlic cloves
1 red pepper, deseeded and cut into large chunks
4 tomatoes, quartered
325 g (12 oz) mixed vegetables, cut into bite-size chunks –
  potatoes, courgette, beans, aubergine
4 tbsp olive oil

Heat half the oil in a large frying pan and brown the sausages.
Place the remaining olive oil into a large roasting tin and add all
of the vegetables and sausages, ensuring they are covered in the
oil. Place in a preheated oven at 200°C (400°F, Gas mark 6) and
cook for 25 minutes or until the vegetables are tender and the
sausages cooked through.

Sprinkle with Parmesan cheese and serve.

Sweetcorn relish

Makes 1.5 kg (3 lb)

6 large fresh corn cobs
½ small white cabbage, finely shredded
2 small onions, finely sliced
475 ml (16 fl oz) malt vinegar
200 g (7 oz) granulated sugar
1 red pepper, finely chopped
1 tbsp plain flour
1 tsp salt
1 tsp mustard powder (optional)
½ tsp turmeric

Put the corn in a pan of boiling water and cook for 2 minutes. Drain and, when cool enough to handle, use a sharp knife to remove the kernels from the cobs.

Place the corn kernels, cabbage and onion in a pan. Reserve 2 tbsp of vinegar and put the rest in the pan. Add the sugar and slowly bring to the boil, stirring occasionally until the sugar dissolves. Simmer for 15 minutes, add the red pepper, and simmer for a further 10 minutes.

Blend the flour, salt, mustard and turmeric with the reserved vinegar to make a smooth paste. Stir the paste into the vegetable mixture. Bring the mixture back to the boil, and then simmer for 5 minutes until the mixture thickens.

Spoon the relish into warmed, sterilized jars, cover and seal. Use within 6 months of making. Once opened, store in the refrigerator and use within 8 weeks.

Tomato base for Bolognese sauce and pizza bases

Makes 500 g (1 lb)

1 onion, chopped
Crushed garlic to taste (optional)
1 kg (2 lb) tomatoes, skinned and chopped
Sweet peppers, chopped (optional)
100 ml (4 fl oz) red wine (optional)
2 tbsp tomato purée or tomato ketchup (optional)
3 tbsp vegetable or olive oil

Heat sufficient oil in a heavy-based frying pan or saucepan to gently fry the onions until soft. Add the crushed garlic and fry for a couple of minutes. Add the chopped tomatoes and sweet peppers and bring to the boil.

Once the mixture has boiled, reduce the heat and simmer to reduce the tomato liquid. Then add the red wine and tomato purée. Stir occasionally. Continue to simmer until the liquid has almost evaporated and the mixture has reduced by at least half. Continue stirring occasionally to prevent the sauce from burning on the bottom of the pan.

Uses for tomato base

The tomato mixture can be added to mince to make Bolognese sauce, to soup, or blended to make a pizza base. (It may need more liquid boiled off and to be blended to make a drier, smoother mix for pizzas.)

Top tip

You may find it easier to make a large batch of tomato base in a preserving pan or large saucepan. This can then be frozen for later use. If the mixture is frozen in muffin or tart tins, the blocks of tomato can be removed from the tins once frozen and stored in freezer bags for later use. Depending on the size of the blocks, you can then defrost just enough for the particular dish you are making.

Tomato chutney, green

Makes 1.25 kg (2.75 lb)

250 g (9 oz) onions, finely chopped
300 ml (10 fl oz) spiced vinegar
250 g (9 oz) apples, peeled, cored and chopped
1 kg (2 lb) green tomatoes, skinned
½ tsp salt
250 g (9 oz) sugar

Cook the chopped onions in a saucepan in a little of the vinegar until nearly soft. Add the rest of the ingredients, apart from the sugar, and enough vinegar to stop the mixture from burning. Cook gently until the tomatoes and apples are soft, stirring from time to time. Add the rest of the vinegar and thoroughly stir in the sugar.

Boil steadily until the chutney is thick, and then pour into warmed, sterilized jars, cover and seal.

Store in a cool dark place.

Tomato and cucumber salad

This recipe is for a simple salad that can be used as an accompaniment to chicken, fish or meat dishes.

Serves 2

2 large or 4 medium tomatoes, or sufficient cherry tomatoes
15 cm (6 inches) of cucumber cut into 1-cm (½-inch) cubes
Lettuce leaves, baby spinach leaves, spicy salad leaves,
*   rocket (or whatever you have available on the allotment)*

For the dressing:

2 tbsp of salad or olive oil
1 tbsp of cider or white wine vinegar
1 tsp Dijon mustard to taste
Chopped herbs to taste
Salt and pepper to taste

Cut the tomatoes into bite-size pieces, place in a bowl and add the diced cucumber. Arrange the salad on a bed of lettuce/salad leaves.

To make the dressing, place all of the ingredients into a sealable jar or container and shake until fully mixed.

Pour sufficient dressing to taste onto the salad just before serving.

To make a heartier meal rather than just an accompaniment use whatever is available from the allotment at the time. Any of the following can be added:

Spring onion, sliced; Sweet pepper, diced; Celery; Grated carrot;
Cold potato, diced; Cold cooked peas; Cold cooked sweetcorn
kernels; Salad onions, thinly sliced; Cold cooked French beans
cut into bite-size pieces; Cold cooked broad beans.

Plus any of the following can be added:

Olives; Pasta spirals cooked and left to cool; Tuna; Salmon; Feta
cheese; Chicken pieces; Sausage (German/Kabanossi, etc.);
Boiled egg, quartered.

Tomato and sweet pepper tart

Serves 6

1 kg (2 lb) tomatoes, halved
2 sweet peppers, sliced
250 g (9 oz) puff pastry
60 g (2 oz) grated cheese
2 tbsp olive oil
1 garlic clove, crushed
Fresh or dried parsley, thyme and oregano to taste
Freshly ground pepper to taste
50g (2 oz) black olives, chopped

Place the tomatoes and peppers on a wire rack in a baking dish and bake for 25–30 minutes until soft.

Roll out the puff pastry to approximately 5 mm (¹/₄ inch) thick and place in a non-stick flan tin, moulding it to the rim around the edge.

Spread the surface of the pastry with the cheese and top with the tomatoes and peppers. Put the olive oil, garlic, herbs and black pepper to taste into a bowl and combine. Sprinkle the mixture over the tart and add the olives.

Bake in the oven at 200°C (400°F, Gas mark 6) for 15–20 minutes. Cut into slices and serve hot or warm.

Vegetable casserole

Serves 6

4 courgettes cut into 1-cm (½-inch) lengths
2 red or green peppers, seeded and chopped
2 onions, roughly chopped
2 carrots, thinly sliced
1 small cauliflower, cut into florets
4 tomatoes, skinned, seeded and chopped
100 g (4 oz) peas
2 tsp paprika
500 ml (18 fl oz) stock
Salt and pepper to taste

Place all the prepared vegetables into a large pan and stir in the spices, seasoning and stock. Bring to the boil and cook on high for 30–40 minutes or until the vegetables are cooked, stirring occasionally.

Vegetable cassoulet

Serves 6

125 g (4 oz) haricot beans
1.4 litres (50 fl oz) water
2 garlic cloves, crushed
225 g (8 oz) shallots, halved, or use 2 medium onions,
  quartered
2 carrots, peeled and diced
1 red pepper, deseeded and chopped
2 courgettes, trimmed and sliced
200 g (7 oz) tomatoes, chopped
1 tbsp each of chopped rosemary, sage and thyme
50 g (2 oz) fresh breadcrumbs
1 tbsp chopped parsley
2 tbsp olive oil
Salt and pepper to taste

Soak the beans overnight, drain and rinse. Place in a saucepan with the water and bring to the boil. Boil rapidly for 10 minutes, reduce the heat and simmer gently for a further 45 minutes. Drain the beans, reserving 300 ml (10 fl oz) of the liquid.

Heat 1 tbsp of the oil in a flameproof casserole dish and add the garlic, shallots/onions, carrot and red pepper. Cook gently for 5 minutes and then add the courgette and tomato and cook for a further 5 minutes. Stir in the beans and reserved water. Add the chopped rosemary, sage and thyme and season to taste.

Mix together the breadcrumbs and parsley with the remaining 1 tbsp of oil. Scatter the mixture evenly over the top of the cassoulet. Cover the casserole dish loosely with foil and transfer to a preheated oven at 190°C (375°F, Gas mark 5) and cook for 30 minutes. Remove the foil and cook for a further 15–20 minutes until the topping is crisp and golden.

Vegetable curry

Serves 4

100–115 g (4 oz) each of carrots, turnips, potatoes, peas,
   broad beans, sweetcorn, cauliflower (or whatever you have
   available on the allotment at the time)
1 large onion, chopped
2 garlic cloves, pounded to a paste
115 ml (4 oz) natural yoghurt
1 green chilli, chopped
3 tbsp vegetable oil
Salt and pepper to taste

Spices:
1 tsp ground cinnamon
1 tsp cumin seeds
1 tsp fennel seeds
1 tsp fenugreek seeds
1 tsp turmeric
1 tsp chilli powder
1 tsp ground coriander
1 tsp garam masala

Peel and chop all the vegetables, apart from the onion, into bite-size cubes, and blanch in boiling water for a few minutes.

Heat the oil and cook the onions on a low heat until golden brown.

Mix the garlic with the yoghurt and add to the onions. Cook for a further 5 minutes on moderate heat, then add all the spices and continue cooking for a further 5 minutes.

Add all the vegetables including the chopped chilli and cook for a further 10–15 minutes, then simmer for a further 5 minutes. Season to taste.

Top tip

If time is short or you do not have a supply of spices, parboil the vegetables until they are almost cooked and then add a ready-made curry paste.

Vegetable lasagne

Serves 4

175 g (6 oz) French beans, chopped
1 large onion, peeled and thinly chopped
400 g (14 oz) tomatoes, skinned and chopped
50 g (2 oz) peas or sweetcorn
1 carrot, peeled and diced
Pinch of oregano or basil
1 packet of cheese sauce mix
100 g (4 oz) lasagne, cooked (or use a variety that does not
*   require pre-cooking)*
50 g (2 oz) grated cheese
2 tbsp olive or vegetable oil
Water as necessary
Salt and pepper to taste

Heat the oil in a saucepan and fry the beans and onion for 5 minutes. Season to taste. Add the tomatoes, peas or sweetcorn, carrot, and oregano or basil, and bring to the boil. Simmer for 20 minutes, adding water as necessary to keep the mixture moist but not wet.

Make up the cheese sauce mix to the manufacturer's instructions. Spread half of the vegetable mixture in a 1.2-litre (2-pint) ovenproof dish and cover with one-third of the lasagne. Spread half the cheese sauce on top, then cover with another layer of lasagne. Spread the remaining vegetable mixture on top, cover with the remaining lasagne, and add the remaining cheese sauce. Sprinkle over the grated cheese and bake at 180°C (350°F, Gas mark 4) for 40 minutes.

Vegetable risotto

Serves 4

100 g (4 oz) asparagus tips, cut into bite-size pieces
50 g (2 oz) peas and/or French beans
50 g (2 oz) baby carrots, diced
1 medium onion, peeled and finely chopped
200 g (8 oz) risotto rice
900 ml (32 fl oz) hot chicken or vegetable stock
75 g (3 oz) grated cheese (preferably Parmesan or a vegetarian
  alternative)
3 tbsp olive oil
Salt and pepper to taste

Boil the vegetables in a small pan of water and cook for 3–5 minutes until tender. Drain and keep warm.

In a large frying pan heat the oil over a medium heat, add the onion and cook for 2–3 minutes until the onion has softened and is translucent. Add the rice and cook for a further 2 minutes, but do not allow it to brown.

Start adding the hot stock to the rice, a ladleful at a time, and bring to the boil, stirring continuously. When the stock is absorbed, add the next ladleful of stock and continue stirring. When half of the stock has been used up, add the vegetables and continue until all of the stock is used and the rice is tender. Ensure each addition of stock is absorbed before adding the next. Continue stirring. Cooking takes 20–25 minutes. Season to taste.

Stir in half of the grated cheese and serve topped with the remainder of the cheese.

Top tip
If using stock cubes, taste the risotto before adding any seasoning.

Top tip
As an alternative, the risotto could also be made with diced chicken, smoked fish or seafood.

Vegetable soup

Serves 4

2 medium onions, chopped
2 leeks, sliced
2 carrots, diced
2 medium potatoes, diced
2 small courgettes, sliced or diced
200 g (7 oz) green beans cut into 2-cm (¾-inch) pieces
2 tomatoes (optional)
1 litre (35 fl oz) water
1 tbsp olive or vegetable oil
Herbs to taste
Salt and pepper to taste

Cook the onions, leeks and herbs in the oil for approximately 5 minutes until the onions are soft. Add the carrots and potatoes and stir. Cook for a further 5 minutes and add the courgettes, green beans, tomatoes (if using), water and herbs, and bring to the boil. Simmer for 30 minutes or until the vegetables are soft, and then check the seasoning.

Additions

You could add 100 g (4 oz) of pasta shapes to the soup 15 minutes before cooking time finishes.

Vegetable stir-fry

Serves 4

350 g (12 oz) mixed vegetables, such as baby sweetcorn or
 sweetcorn cut into 3-cm (1-inch) pieces, red pepper
 deseeded, broccoli florets, baby carrots, mangetout peas,
 leeks
2 tsp Dijon mustard
1 tbsp lemon juice
2 tbsp olive oil

Slice the vegetables into small, even-size pieces. Heat the oil in a
large frying pan or wok and when hot add the prepared
vegetables (except the pepper and mangetout) and fry for
5 minutes. Add the pepper and mangetout and fry for a further
3 minutes.

Stir in the mustard and lemon juice and heat through. Serve
immediately with noodles or rice.

Vegetable stock

2 large onions, chopped
2 large carrots, chopped
1 bunch celery, chopped
1 bunch parsley, chopped
You may also include cabbage leaves, cauliflower stalks, leeks
    and parsnips
½ tsp black peppercorns
2.5 litres (90 fl oz) cold water, lightly salted

Place all the ingredients and the cold water in a large saucepan. Boil over a medium heat, then reduce the heat and simmer over a low heat, stirring occasionally, for 30 minutes. Remove the pan from the heat and allow to cool.

Strain the stock through muslin or a sieve, and use as required.

Top tip

The stock can also be frozen in ice-cube trays and the blocks stored in freezer bags. The blocks can then be used as required.

Gardening terms

Acid soil A soil that is lime-free with a pH value of less than 7.

Aerate Loosen soil to alter its texture and structure to allow air to be incorporated.

Alkaline soil A soil that contains a large amount of calcium (lime) and has a pH value above 7.

Annual plant A plant that grows from seed, then flowers and dies within one season.

Ballerina Upright columnar tree with short fruiting spurs close to the trunk. Ideal for narrow spaces.

Bare-rooted plant A plant sold with no soil around its roots.

Bedding plant A plant that is planted out in quantity mainly for one season.

Biennial plant A plant that grows from seed in one year, and flowers or fruits, sets seeds and dies in the following year.

Biological control Controlling pests, diseases or weeds by using natural enemies such as predators, parasites and pathogens.

Bolt (Run to seed) To produce flowers and seeds prematurely.

Brassica Member of the cabbage family.

Bud An unopened flower or condensed shoot.

Bush A tree pruned to give up to 80 cm (32 inches) of clear stem.

Cane A long and slender shoot produced from the crown of a plant. Also a stick to support plants.

Chicons White, compact, and plump leafy heads produced from the roots of chicory, which have been grown in the dark during winter.

Cloche A low transparent cover designed to protect plants during the early stages of their growth.

Compost Decomposed vegetable or animal matter; peat or peat alternative, or sterilized soil, used for sowing seeds and cuttings.

Cordon A tree trained vertically or at an angle, with the main stem pruned to produce fruiting spurs.

Cross Seeds produced by cross-pollination of two or more parent plants.

Culinary Used for cooking or processing rather than eaten fresh.

Cultivar Cultivated variety that originated in cultivation and not in the wild.

Current year's growth Shoots that have grown in the current season.

Cutting A piece of stem cut from a plant for propagation.

Dessert Suitable for eating fresh and uncooked (e.g. apples, gooseberries and plums).

Double digging Digging to a depth of two spades without bringing the subsoil to the surface.

Earthing up Drawing soil towards the stems of plants, such as potatoes, leeks and celery, to encourage more growth or to exclude light to blanch the stems. If growing potatoes are exposed to light, the tubers will become green, bitter and poisonous. Earthing up will prevent this from happening.

Espalier A tree trained to form a vertical trunk, with pairs of branches trained horizontally in a series of tiers.

Fan A tree trained to form a series of branches spreading like the ribs of a fan.

Fertile soil Soil capable of producing a good crop.

Foliar feed Applying a liquid fertilizer by watering or spraying onto the plant leaves.

Forcing Induce plant growth by controlling light levels.

Germination The emergence of a root and shoot from a seed.

Green manure A leafy crop grown for the purpose of digging it into the soil. The crop takes in nitrates that would otherwise be washed away with winter rains, which are then released by the decaying crop.

Hardening off Gradual acclimatization of a plant, raised under cover, to outside temperatures.

Heeling in Temporary planting of a plant in a trench, pending a permanent position.

Humus Generally applied to partly decomposed organic material incorporated into the soil.

Hybrid Plants with genetically distinct parents.

Inorganic A chemical or fertilizer that is not obtained from something that has been alive.

Insecticide A chemical used to control insect pests.

Interplanting/intercropping A practical way of increasing production by planting quicker maturing plants, such as lettuce and radish, between slower growing crops, or by growing a row of plants between the rows of unrelated crops.

Maiden A one-year-old tree.

Mulch A layer of organic materials placed around plants.

Nematodes Microscopic worm-like animals used as pest predators.

Neutral soil Soil with a pH value of 7 that is neither acid nor alkaline.

Offset Young plant that is produced naturally by the parent plant at its base.

Organic Obtained from a source that was once alive.

Pathogen An organism that causes a disease in another organism. Pathogens include fungi, bacteria and viruses.

Peat Decomposed plant matter obtained from boggy ground.

Perennial plant A plant that is capable of living more than three years.

pH The measure of acidity in the soil.

Pinching out The removal of a growing tip.

Pollination The application of pollen to a flower.

Pot-bound When the roots of a plant have filled a pot completely, leaving no more room for them to grow.

Pricking out Transferring a seedling or rooted cutting into another container.

Propagation Reproduction or multiplication of plants.

Pruning Removing parts of a plant to improve shape or production of fruit.

Puddle in Soaking the soil around a plant until a puddle forms.

Root crop Plants where the swollen root is eaten.

Rootstock A more vigorous root to which another shoot or stem is grafted.

Runner A shoot produced by the parent plant that runs along the soil rooting at intervals.

Species Plants that are genetically similar.

Spit The depth of a spade, approximately 23 cm (9 inches).

Spur A short twiggy branch that bears fruit buds.

Successional sowing Making a number of small sowings of seeds at regular intervals so that a continuous supply of vegetables is produced without causing a glut.

Systemic A chemical, insecticide, fungicide or weedkiller that is absorbed by the plant and travels in the sap to other parts of the plant, including the roots. The advantages of using such products is that it is not necessary to cover the whole plant with the chemical to obtain a good result, and systemic insecticides are less likely to harm beneficial insects that do not feed on the plant. The disadvantages are that some systemic chemicals nay remain for some time and may render a crop unusable until they have dispersed or decomposed.

Tilth The crumbly structure of soil.

Trace element A chemical that plants only need in small amounts.

Transplanting Movement of a plant from one position to another.

Variety A variation of a species.

Vegetative growth The development of stems and leaves.

Vegetative production Reproduction by cuttings, division or layering.

Virus A microscopic organism that is capable of causing malformation or disease of a plant.

Pests

Allium leaf miner Discovered in the West Midlands in 2003 on allotment and garden crops, affecting leeks and onions. The larvae eat their way into the leaves and bulbs, causing bacterial and fungal infections such as white rot. Can be controlled by delaying planting until after April when the first threat of adult emergence has passed. Cover the crop with fleece to prevent the adults laying eggs. Treat with an appropriate systemic insecticide in March/April and October. Not to be confused with the leek moth.

Aphid Usually green, black or grey insects approximately 2 mm (1/8 inch) in length. Aphid affects most plants, although some (lupin aphid) are plant-specific. Aphid causes damage to crops by sucking the sap, which can also introduce viruses. Affected plants show reduced growth and leaf damage. Can be controlled to some extent by spraying with soapy water or rubbing off with the fingers; alternatively, spray with an appropriate insecticide.

Asparagus beetle Will strip the leaves and eat the spears. Pick them off by hand or spray with pyrethrum natural insecticide. Burn old stems at the end of the year to kill over-wintering beetles.

Blackfly Member of the aphid family, usually seen on the shoot tips of broad beans. Affected plants are weakened and the bean pods fail to develop. Can be controlled by pinching out the tips of fully grown plants and treating as for aphid.

Cabbage root fly Maggots, up to 9 mm (1/2 inch) long, cause damage by eating the roots, which causes the stems to rot. Place a collar of fleece, carpet underlay or cardboard around seedlings to prevent the fly from laying its eggs.

Cabbage white butterflies They lay their eggs on brassicas, and the emerging caterpillars eat holes in the leaves. Control by covering the crop, if possible, with fine netting to prevent the butterflies from laying eggs. Pick off or squash the caterpillars or spray with a suitable insecticide.

Carrot fly Creamy yellow maggots, 9 mm (1/2 inch) long, eat their way into the carrot causing rusty brown lines on the outside of the roots. The damage caused may eventually lead to infection, causing the carrot to rot. Carrot fly is attracted by the smell of the carrots, so avoid disturbing the carrots as much as possible. Try interplanting rows of onions to confuse the smell. Alternatively, protect the crop with horticultural fleece or construct a physical barrier by fencing with clear plastic or fleece to a height of 60 cm (24 inches) as carrot flies do not fly higher than 45 cm (18 inches).

Celery leaf miner The white maggots, 7 mm (¼ inch) long, eat the insides of leaves, producing thin bitter-tasting stems. Destroy all affected leaves.

Flea beetle Small beetles 2 mm ($^1/_8$ inch) long that eat small round holes in plant leaves. Heavy attacks can kill seedlings. Spray with an appropriate insecticide if the infestation is heavy.

Leek moth Caterpillars, 12 mm (½ inch) long, tunnel their way inside the stems of onions, shallots and leeks, causing damage and secondary rotting. Remove and destroy badly affected leaves and plants or spray with an appropriate insecticide.

Lettuce root aphid Creamy yellow aphid, 2 mm ($^1/_8$ inch) long, feed on the roots, causing the lettuce to wilt. Treat with an appropriate insecticide.

Onion fly Maggots, up to 8 mm ($^1/_2$ inch) long, burrow into the base of the onion, eating the roots and allowing secondary damage that causes the onion to rot. Young plants are frequently killed and older ones fail to develop. Destroy plants before the maggots go into the soil to pupate. Keep well watered.

Pea and bean weevil Greyish-brown beetles, 3–4 mm ($^1/_8$ inch) long, feed on the leaf margins and can retard seedlings, but are rarely fatal. Spray with an appropriate insecticide.

Pea moth They lay their eggs in the pea flower. Caterpillars hatch inside the pod and eat the peas. Spray with an appropriate insecticide just after flowers form.

Red spider mite Tiny mites that mainly affect crops grown under cover – they feed on the leaves, which curl, turn brown and die. The first signs are mottling of the leaves followed by fine webs. Red spider mites prefer dry conditions so plants need to be mist-sprayed twice a day and the greenhouse damped down to increase humidity. Can be controlled with insecticidal soap or appropriate insecticide.

Slugs and snails The bane of all gardeners as they eat most crops. There are several species, some of which live entirely under the soil. They shelter under stones and debris during the day and feed at night, and they are active throughout the year. They feed whenever the temperature is above freezing. For prevention, ensure your plot is kept clean and hiding places are removed. Encourage frogs and toads into your garden or plot. Create barriers by surrounding plants with slug-repellent materials such as sharp sand or grit, ash or sawdust. Use copper wire to protect individual plants, pots and raised beds. Protect young plants with cloches. Go out at night with a torch and pick the slugs or snails off for disposal by dropping them in a bucket of salty water. Shallow traps consisting of half beer and half water can be set at soil level, and will attract and drown slugs. If using a commercial slug bait, place under black polythene or a flower pot to avoid harming birds and animals. Slugs can also be controlled by biological methods such as the use of nematodes.

Whitefly Clouds of small white sap-sucking insects affecting all brassicas or greenhouse crops such as cucumbers and tomatoes. Treat with an appropriate insecticide.

Diseases

Blight Affects both potatoes and tomatoes, particularly if the weather is warm and wet. Potato blight is a fungus spread by wind and rain. The leaves of affected plants develop brown patches and the leaves collapse and die. Infected tubers (potatoes) develop dark patches on the skin with a reddish-brown discoloration beneath. The discoloration may then spread to the flesh, turning it into a smelly, slimy wet rot that destroys the potato. At the first sign of symptoms, cut off and destroy the foliage to prevent spores from washing into the soil and affecting the tubers. Affected tomato plants should be destroyed. Blight can be prevented by spraying with a copper-based fungicide, especially if the weather is wet and warm. Do not compost affected plants. Grow potato varieties that show some blight resistance, for example, Arran Pilot, Cara, Foremost, Maris Peer, Pentland Crown, Romano.

Blossom end rot Affects tomatoes and is caused by erratic watering in which the plant dries out and cannot absorb enough calcium. The end of the affected tomato goes brown and leathery. Ensure an adequate supply of water at all times. If blossom end rot does develop, pick off affected fruits and improve the watering.

Clubroot A serious problem that affects brassicas. It is caused by a fungus that attacks roots and kills them, causing the plant to wilt or die, or produce a poor crop. The spores can remain in the soil for many years, and a number of allotment sites are badly affected. Preventative measures should be taken by ensuring crop rotation and burning affected plants. Be careful not to spread the spores around the plot on tools or boots, or by moving the infected soil. If the site is prone to clubroot, seeds should be sown in modules, not directly into the soil, and should be planted out when they are sufficiently established to be less vulnerable. Liming the soil before planting will also deter it and improve the soil conditions.

Damping off Can affect all young seedlings. Roots and stem bases rot and the seedlings collapse and die. It is caused by a fungus that spreads rapidly in damp, poorly ventilated conditions, or where hygiene is poor. Prevent infection by sowing seeds in clean pots and trays with fresh potting compost. Only water with mains water, not water collected in a water butt. Spraying with a copper-based fungicide may also help prevent infection.

Onion white rot Causes leaves to turn yellow and wilt. Fluffy white fungus is visible at the roots and bulb bases. This is a serious problem and affected plants must be destroyed. There is no chemical control available and further crops should not be grown in the same spot for at least seven years.

Common fruit problems

Apple canker A serious disease in apples and pears in which the bark shrinks and cracks. Cut off any damaged twigs and also cut out any cankers from the stems and branches and paint with a wound paint. Canker is caused by a fungus that is spread by wind-borne spores that enter through wounded areas such as pruning cuts, frost cracks or other wounds, or by attacks by woolly aphid. Keep the trees pruned to encourage new and unaffected growth.

Codling moth Small white caterpillars bore into the developing fruit and feed on the core. They have usually finished feeding, and tunnelled out of the apple, by the time it is ripe, ready to overwinter in the tree bark. Pheromone traps attract the males, reducing mating, but also indicate when the moth is active, allowing spraying with an appropriate insecticide when the adults are active and laying eggs.

Gooseberry mildew Also known as American gooseberry mildew, this affects gooseberries and also blackcurrants.

Powdery grey/white fungal growth appears on upper leaves, stems and fruit. Severely affected leaves and shoot tips may die off. The affected fruits are still edible but can be unsightly. Control by pruning out affected branches as soon as they are seen, and thin the growth to encourage better air circulation through the plant. Spray with an appropriate fungicide.

Gooseberry sawfly The pale caterpillar-like larvae, up to 20 mm (¾ inch) long, eat the leaves and severely defoliate the bushes, which often results in bare stems by the time the berries are ready for harvesting. Spray affected plants with an appropriate insecticide at the first signs of damage.

Grey mould Affects strawberries, raspberries and currants, particularly in a wet summer. The fruits develop normally but then are covered by a grey mould. Numerous spores are released when the fruit is picked. The spores are spread by rain, water splashes and on air currents. Fruits that have been damaged, for example by birds or slugs, may also become infected. Control is difficult. Remove all dead and injured parts of the plant before they become infected. Spray with a suitable fungicide in humid weather to prevent infection.

taking it further

Associations and organizations

British Beekeepers' Association
The National Bee Centre
National Agricultural Centre
Stoneleigh Park
Warwickshire CV8 2LG
Tel: 02476 696679
www.britishbee.org.uk

Centre for Alternative Technology
Machynlleth
Powys SY20 9AZ
Tel: 01654 705950
www.cat.org.uk

Promotes ideas and information on technologies that support rather than damage the environment.

Garden Organic (Henry Doubleday Research Association – HDRA)
Ryton
Coventry
Warwickshire CV8 3LG
Tel: 02476 303517
www.gardenorganic.org.uk

National charity for organic growing.

National Allotment Gardens Trust
PO Box 1448
Marston
Oxford OX3 3AY
Tel: 01752 363379
www.nagtrust.org

The National Society of Allotment and Leisure Gardeners Ltd
O'Dell House
Hunters Road
Corby
Northants NN17 5JE
Tel: 01536 266576
Email: natsoc@nsalg.org.uk
www.nsalg.org.uk

Permaculture Association
BCM Permaculture Association
London WC1N 3XX
Tel: 0845 4581805
www.permaculture.org.uk

Supports people and projects using the ethics and principles of permaculture.

Royal Horticultural Society
80 Vincent Square
London SW1P 2PE
Tel: 0845 2605000
www.rhs.org.uk

Royal Society for the Prevention of Cruelty to Animals (RSPCA)
RSPCA Enquiries Service
Wilberforce Way
Southwater
Horsham
West Sussex RH13 9RS
Tel: 0300 1234555
www.rspca.org.uk

Soil Association
South Plaza
Marlborough Street
Bristol BS1 3NX
Tel: 0117 3145000
www.soilassociation.org

Campaigns for organic food and farming.

Thrive
The Geoffrey Udall Centre
Beech Hill
Reading RG7 2AT
Tel: 0118 9885688
www.thrive.org.uk

Aims to enable positive change in the lives of people with disabilities through horticulture.

Government departments

Department of Communities and Local Government (DCLG)
Elland House
Bressenden Place
London SW1E 5DU
Tel: 020 7944 4400
www.communities.gov.uk

This department is responsible for allotments.

Department of Farming and Rural Affairs (DEFRA)
Customer Contact Unit
Eastbury House
30–34 Albert Embankment
London SE1 7TL
Tel: 0845 9335577
www.defra.gov.uk

Government Office for the West Midlands
5 St Philip's Place
Colmore Row
Birmingham B3 2PW
Tel: 0121 3525050
www.go-wm.gov.uk

Responsible for applications to dispose of allotments.

Livestock, hens, poultry equipment and information

www.chickenkeeper.co.uk

www.happychicks.co.uk (Suppliers of ex-battery hens)

www.pandtpoultry.co.uk

www.animalloversweb.com

www.thepigsite.com

www.petsamaritans.co.uk

www.smallholder.co.uk

Magazines

Garden News
www.gardeningmags.co.uk

Grow Your Own
www.growfruitandveg.co.uk

Kitchen Garden
www.kitchengarden.co.uk

Pesticides

Chemical disposal service finder

Enter your postcode on the site to find where your nearest chemical disposal service is located

www.chem-away.org.uk

Crop Protection Association

www.garden-care.org.uk

Information on common-sense gardening.

Health and Safety Executive

www.hse.gov.uk

Pesticides Action Network
Development House
56–64 Leonard Street
London EC2A 4LT
Tel: 020 7065 0905
www.pan-uk.org

Working to eliminate the dangers of toxic pesticides and exposure to them.

Pesticides Safety Directorate

www.pesticides.gov.uk/garden_home.asp

This is the government department responsible for the approval of pesticides. This site can be used to find a suitable pesticide or check whether chemicals in your possession are still authorized for use.

Seed companies and plant suppliers

D. T. Brown
Bury Road
Newmarket CB8 7QB
Tel: 0845 3710532
www.dtbrownseeds.co.uk

Dobies
Long Road
Paignton
Devon TQ4 7SX
Tel: 0844 7017623
www.dobies.co.uk

E. W. King & Co
Monks Farm
Pantlings Lane
Coggeshall Road
Kelvedon
Essex CO5 9PG
Tel: 01376 570000
www.kingsseeds.com

Marshalls
S. E. Marshall & Co
Alconbury Hill
Huntingdon
Cambridgeshire PE28 4HY
Tel: 01480 443390
www.marshalls-seeds.co.uk

Ken Muir
Rectory Road
Weeley Heath
Clacton on Sea
Essex CO16 9BJ
Tel: 01255 830181
www.kenmuir.co.uk

Seeds of Italy
C3 Phoenix Industrial Estate
Rosslyn Crescent
Harrow
Middlesex HA1 2SP
Tel: 020 8427 5020
www.seedsofitaly.com

Suffolk Herbs
Monks Farm
Kelvedon
Essex CO5 9PG
Tel: 01376 572456
www.suffolkherbs.com

Suttons
Suttons Consumer Products Ltd
Woodview Road
Paignton
Devon TQ4 7NG
Tel: 0844 9222899
www.suttons.co.uk

Thompson & Morgan
Poplar Lane
Ipswich
Suffolk IP8 3BU
Tel: 01473 695200
www.thompson-morgan.com

Equipment suppliers

Ascott Smallholding Supplies Ltd
Units 9/10 The Old Creamery
Four Crosses
Llanymynech SY22 6LP
Tel: 0845 1306285
www.ascott.biz

Glass jars, horticultural and poultry supplies.

Harrod UK Ltd
Pinbush Road
Lowestoft
Suffolk NR33 7NL
Tel: 0845 2185301
www.harrodhorticultural.com

Kits for making raised beds, also traps and nematodes.

Lakeland (Plastics)

www.lakeland.co.uk

Kitchenware and storage solutions – there are shops
nationwide.

LBS Horticulture Ltd
Standroyd Mill
Cottontree
Colne
Lancashire BB8 7BW
Fax: 01282 869850
Email: sales@lbs-group.co.uk
www.lbsgardenwarehouse.co.uk

Suppliers of horticultural requisites and bulk purchase.

Further reading

Clevely, A. (2008) *The Allotment Book*, Collins.

Crouch, D. and Ward, C (1997) *The Allotment: Its Landscape and Culture*, Mushroom Books.

Foley, C. (2008) *Practical Allotment Gardening*, New Holland.

Leendertz, L. (2006) *The Half-Hour Allotment*, Royal Horticultural Society.

Nicol, A. (2007) *The Allotment Gardener's Cookbook*, Silverdale Books.

Reader's Digest (2007) *The Allotment Gardener's Cookbook*.

Roberts, V. (2006) *Teach Yourself Keeping Chickens*, Hodder Education.

York, T. (2007) *Teach Yourself Keeping Pigs*, Hodder Education.

basic gardening skills

jane mcmorland hunter & chris kelly

- Are you clueless about where to start in your garden?
- Do you need to know what to do and when?
- Would you like guidance on growing your own vegetables?

Designed for the complete beginner, **Basic Gardening Skills** shows you how to turn a patch of muddy ground into an easily manageable, sustainable garden, whatever the size of your plot and however busy you are. From creating patios and growing vegetables to dealing with drought, it is packed with easy-to-follow, practical advice.

Jane McMorland Hunter is a passionate gardener and published author. **Chris Kelly** is an experienced gardener and professional writer. Both have many years' experience designing, constructing and maintaining a variety of gardens.

teach
yourself

growing your own fruit and veg
michael thurlow

- Do you need help to decide what to grow?
- Do you have a small garden, or limited space?
- Would you like a fun and rewarding hobby for the family?

Growing Your Own Fruit and Veg provides comprehensive advice for anyone wishing to grow fresh produce. You will find specific instructions and step-by-step guides on when, where and how to grow and maintain fruit and vegetables, without the use of chemicals. An A–Z list of plants together with advice on ease of growth and a family-friendly approach make this an essential guide to enjoying your own produce.

Michael Thurlow is head gardener at Audley End Organic Kitchen Garden, which yields organic produce all year round.

teach
yourself

beekeeping
adrian and claire waring

- Would you like to produce your own honey?
- Do you need information about equipment?
- Would you like advice on seasonal needs?

Whether you are simply curious, or are an amateur beekeeper already, **Beekeeping** will teach you everything you need to know. From bee biology to the best hives for town or country bees, covering courses, upkeep and even dealing with the neighbours, this friendly introduction has information on taking your hobby further and also includes some great honey recipes.

Adrian and Claire Waring have over 65 years of beekeeping experience between them. Both are former General Secretaries of the British Beekeepers' Association. Adrian is a former County Bee Instructor and Examiner and Claire is Editor of *Bee Craft*.

teach yourself

keeping chickens
victoria roberts

- Do you want to know which breed lays best?
- Would you like advice on housing and equipment?
- Are you considering keeping ducks and geese?

Whether you want to start from scratch with a few hens, or branch into ducks, geese and other birds, **Keeping Chickens** is for you. It tells you which breed of bird lays best and gives useful guidance on housing, equipment and the necessities of day-to-day care. Covering all types of poultry, this guide offers advice on everything from exhibiting birds to meat production, with a full 'trouble-shooting' section and even tips for breeding your birds.

Victoria Roberts, BVSc MRCVS, is the author or editor of five books on keeping poultry, the Honorary Veterinary Surgeon for the Poultry Club, and the editor of the Poultry Club newsletter.

teach yourself	**keeping pigs** tony york

- Do you want to know which breed is right for you?
- Would you like advice on housing and equipment?
- Do you want guidelines on how to spot disease or illness?

If you are already a pig keeper or perhaps a would-be 'hobby farmer' keen to experience the 'good life', **Keeping Pigs** is for you. It will give you everything you need to keep happy and healthy pigs, from practical instructions on which equipment you'll need, to information on feeding and maintenance and guidelines on meat production. It also has lots of useful resources, including a gestation calendar, and plenty of helpful contacts.

Tony York is a pig farmer whose courses on pig-keeping have attracted people from across the UK for over 15 years.